LIFESTYLES

In the modern world our lifestyle helps to define our attitudes and values as well as show our wealth and social position. This clearly written introduction to the concept of lifestyle offers a concise guide to how the term is used in sociological accounts to refer to this modern social form. *Lifestyles* explores how we should classify lifestyles, why they have become more important and what precisely constitutes a lifestyle.

Organised into four parts, the first places the development of lifestyles in the context of modern society, and shows how lifestyles and consumerism have generated a wide range of research on the use of consumer goods to distinguish identities. The second reviews the work of a number of social theorists who have attempted to explain the meanings of fashionable style in modern culture. The third explains the characteristic themes of lifestyles such as surfaces, selves and sensibilities, while the final part offers a view on the aestheticisation of everyday life.

By reviewing a wide range of published material, introducing central themes in the sociology of modern life, examining distinctive styles in social theory and offering its own original contribution to current debates, *Lifestyles* provides students with a much needed overview of this often misused term.

David Chaney is Professor of Sociology at the University of Durham.

KEY IDEAS
Series Editor: Peter Hamilton
The Open University

KEY IDEAS
Series Editor: PETER HAMILTON
The Open University, Milton Keynes

Designed to complement the successful *Key Sociologists*, this series covers the main concepts, issues, debates and controversies in sociology and the social sciences. The series aims to provide authoritative essays on central topics of social science, such as community, power, work, sexuality, inequality, benefits and ideology, class, family, etc. Books adopt a strong individual 'line' constituting original essays rather than literary surveys and form lively and original treatments of their subject matter. The books will be useful to students and teachers of sociology, political science, economics, psychology, philosophy and geography.

THE SYMBOLIC CONSTRUCTION OF COMMUNITY
ANTHONY P. COHEN, Department of Social Anthropology, University of Manchester
SOCIETY
DAVID FRISBY and DEREK SAYER, Department of Sociology, University of Manchester
SEXUALITY
JEFFREY WEEKS, Social Work Studies Department, University of Southampton
WORKING
GRAEME SALAMAN, Faculty of Social Sciences, The Open University, Milton Keynes
BELIEFS AND IDEOLOGY
KENNETH THOMPSON, Faculty of Social Sciences, The Open University, Milton Keynes
EQUALITY
BRYAN TURNER, School of Social Sciences, The Flinders University of South Australia
HEGEMONY
ROBERT BOCOCK, Faculty of Social Sciences, The Open University, Milton Keynes
RACISM
ROBERT MILES, Department of Sociology, University of Glasgow
POSTMODERNITY
BARRY SMART, Associate Professor of Sociology, University of Auckland, New Zealand
CLASS
STEPHEN EDGELL, School of Social Sciences, University of Salford
CONSUMPTION
ROBERT BOCOCK, Faculty of Social Sciences, The Open University, Milton Keynes
CULTURE
CHRIS JENKS, Department of Sociology, Goldsmiths' College
MASS MEDIA
PIERRE SORLIN, University of Paris III
GLOBALIZATION
MALCOLM WATERS, University of Tasmania, Australia
CHILDHOOD
CHRIS JENKS, Department of Sociology, Goldsmiths' College

LIFESTYLES

DAVID CHANEY

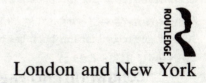

London and New York

First published 1996
by Routledge
11 New Fetter Lane, London EC4P 4EE

Simultaneously published in the USA and Canada
by Routledge
29 West 35th Street, New York, NY 10001

© 1996 David Chaney

Phototypeset by Intype London Ltd

Printed and bound in Great Britain by Clays Ltd, St Ives PLC

British Library Cataloguing in Publication Data
A catalogue record for this book is available from the British Library

Library of Congress Cataloging in Publication Data

A catalogue record for this book has been requested

ISBN 0–415–11718–6 (hbk)
ISBN 0–415–11719–4 (pbk)

This book is for Karina

Contents

Preface

This book is about the concept of lifestyle – how the term is used in sociological accounts to refer to what is seen to be a modern social form. More generally, how and why lifestyles are embedded in a broader theme of a culture of consumerism. I have chosen to tackle this task through three contrasting perspectives, each covered in a part of the book.

My reason for adopting this approach is given by the character of lifestyles. Social research would be a lot easier if the concepts we used stood for (or referred to) distinct, clearly specifiable entities. This is not, however, the normal case so it has become accepted that, particularly in modern societies, social concepts refer rather to 'families'. What I mean by this term is that a number of quite different things or processes are collected together by something they share to give a sense of common identity. That which is shared is usually both an institutional setting and a way of being expressed – a discourse. I will, through the contrasting perspectives of the first three parts, try make clear some of the family of things that the discourse of lifestyle includes.

In the first part I discuss how a sense of lifestyle has been formulated in relation to some primarily empirical accounts of the changing social structures of modernity. In the second part I shift to a discussion of some social theories of the cultural changes of modernity and how a notion of lifestyle has been used in these accounts. In addition to reviewing the relevant literature I try to show the cultural implications of continual innovations in goods and services in mass society. Then in the third part I look more closely at the cultural form of contemporary lifestyles, showing how it tends to use characteristic themes and perspectives. While each of these parts can be read independently I believe that, cumulatively, they delineate a family likeness.

I argue throughout that a sense of a distinctive type of concern (the family that the notion of lifestyle refers to) is used, and has been used, reflexively by social actors. And thus in the modern era lifestyles have developed as projects that they invest with ethical and aesthetic significance. In the fourth and concluding part of the book I take up this aspect more directly through a discussion of how we can see people using lifestyles to, in a sense, design themselves.

This book is part of a broader project of work concerned with the culture of modernity, in particular the changing discourses and representations of collective identities – how we identify ourselves as similar to and different from others. I am less interested in trying to map the various styles of identity than to explore the politics of social knowledge, that is with how various vocabularies of social life express distinctive types of authority and identity. I am as always deeply appreciative of the intellectual culture of my department at the University of Durham, and especially the sympathetic interest of my friends and colleagues in the Sociology of Knowledge and Social Politics research group. In particular, my friends and colleagues Andy Bennett, Nick Ellison and Dick Hobbs have made helpful suggestions on the work in progress.

I have, in relation to previous books, acknowledged my very real appreciation of the stimulus and encouragement that Chris Rojek has provided as editor. He gave me the initial idea for this book and although he subsequently moved on he has continued to encourage and support the project unstintingly. Lots of thanks to him and to Mari Shullaw who has helped to complete the project.

Part I

A modern social form

there are problems in defining something as nebulous as a lifestyle. I could tell you about my own or about others that I am familiar with, but building up instances tells us about social variety rather than what makes a lifestyle or not. In the first part of the book I shall therefore be mainly concerned with the contexts within which we have come to use a notion of lifestyles. In this first chapter I shall discuss lifestyles in the context of notions of social structure, and then in the next look at lifestyles as they have depended upon the development of consumer culture. In the third chapter I will be able to talk more precisely about the purposes to which concepts of lifestyles have been put.

I shall begin with the assumption that lifestyles are features of the modern world or what I shall also call modernity. What this means is that those who live in modern societies will use a notion of lifestyle to describe their own and others' actions. Lifestyles are patterns of action that differentiate people. In everyday interaction we can employ a notion of lifestyle without needing to explain what we mean; and indeed were we to be challenged we might find it difficult to go beyond a halting and very general description of the sorts of things lifestyle refers to. Lifestyles therefore help to make sense of (that is explain but not necessarily justify) what people do, and why they do it, and what doing it means to them and others.

This does not mean to say that lifestyles are relevant to everybody's lives, and we can easily imagine that there will be people (who might call themselves 'real people') who will deny that they have, or might want, a lifestyle. But in general lifestyle can be used in public discourse without needing to be glossed as being difficult or a bit of jargon. Lifestyles are therefore part of the everyday social life of the modern world and, if my initial presupposition is right, they function in interaction in ways that would be incomprehensible to those who do not live in modern society. I shall spend some time explaining why I place lifestyles as features of modernity. I do so because it is an essential prerequisite for later chapters on developments in theorising lifestyles, and because, more prosaically, it helps to give a more specific context for attempts to be explicit about how notions of lifestyle are used.

Distinctive patterns of social life are often summarised by the term culture (there are of course other more artistic meanings of culture but I do not want to take up that issue now). Indeed a culture has been defined as: 'the total life-style of a people – their customs, attitudes, and values, the shared understandings that bind them together as a society' (Kephart 1982, p. 93). I believe this is, however, to misuse the notion of lifestyle. While lifestyles are dependent on cultural forms, each is a style, a manner, a way of using certain goods, places and times that is characteristic of a group but is not the totality of their social experience. Lifestyles are sets of practices and attitudes that make sense in particular contexts. Although I have been careful to write of these styles as ways of using rather than producing things, by the end of the book I will want to overturn the distinction; but initially at least it helpfully clarifies the topic.

Modern social order requires complex machineries of elaborate differentiation and enforcement, as well as modern understandings of citizenship which presume a high degree of individual discipline. Both aspects suggest that it follows that order is *structured* and this can be understood in two ways. The first is that regulations and bureaucratic procedures are an impersonal network of bonds out there; they exist as a framework which operates in ways that are largely impervious to personal circumstance. The second aspect of structure is that a world of bureaucratic government is also a world of them and us. There are those who are able to take decisions influencing organisational goals and practices (or seem to be able to follow what is going on), and those who feel themselves subject to the exercise of others' power.[1] Notions of upper class or elite have been used to refer to those who have the ability to perpetuate their privileges through time and space, although there are inevitably a wide number of ways of measuring social stratification and defining sources of prestige in complex societies (see for example Crompton 1993).

Although class has tended to be emphasised by sociologists, largely because it has been seen to provide the logic of structural order as well as offering a theoretical possibility of transcendent resolution through conflict, other categories of structural identity have been emphasised in specific national circumstances. Most typically various modes of religious or ethnic identification have been used to sustain and explain structured privileges in modern social order. And universally, structures of gendered discrimination, known as patriarchal relationships, have cross-cut and reinforced other forms of oppression.[2] I am here though more concerned with the ways in which the language of forms and styles of status are negotiated. This is largely because there is by now a traditional distinction, following Weber (1966), between status as opposed to class, to indicate a concern with social differences stemming from ways of using rather than producing resources (see Turner 1988). By the language of status I mean the ways in which the inhabitants of modern societies talk about and identify features of the life-worlds of structurally patterned social groupings, and how this discourse informs, shapes and motivates their understanding of the common sense of social order.

The language of social structure is reflexive in every form of society, but the characteristic becomes particularly significant in the social changes of modernity. This is because as the rigidities of established distinction become increasingly hard to sustain in eras of rapid social and physical mobility, new forms of distinction are continually being elaborated and therefore the manner of our concern with and respect for (or repugnance against) the various possible modes of others' civilisation becomes crucial in constituting the normative hierarchies of structured difference. My emphasis upon the language of social structure directs attention to the more general theme of the reflexive character of modernity's endemic concern with social identity, distinction and difference. Bayley has suggested that snobbery and taste are closely interrelated developments of modernity in that both are reactions to the collapse of 'naturally' ordered distinctions: 'Taste is a new religion whose rites are celebrated in department stores and museums, two institutions whose origins lie in exactly that historical period which witnessed the explosion of popular consumption' (1991, p. 209).

Reflexive means here that these social processes are in part constituted through the ways in which they are identified, enacted and responded to. Bayley quotes Furbank on snobbery who said that: ' "in classing someone socially, one is simultaneously classing oneself". He might just as easily have said "in criticizing someone else's taste, one is simultaneously criticizing oneself" ' (1991, p. 6). Bayley goes on to suggest that: 'Snobbery is . . . an institution at least as formidable as the prison system and certainly as characteristic as the age that created it. It can be . . . dated quite precisely to the years when the laws of consumer culture were being established' (1991, p. 70). A suggestion that prompts the further speculation that the by now well-worn metaphor of the panopticon should be supplemented by the dandy as iconic images of modernity.

I want to argue then that, even as the social classes of the modern world were being delineated and institutionalised (in each national context), the contours of distinction were being blurred and elaborated (for a review of the literature on the extent to which social class differences still underlie differences in lifestyle attitudes, behaviours and taste see DiMaggio 1994). These cross-cutting groupings were identified – both by themselves and others – through features of cultural style and sensibility as much as by any more 'material' factors: 'The existence of artificial life-styles, self-consciously created as if they were works of art, suggests a lack of inevitability in the living patterns that classes adopt' (Bensman and Vidich 1995, p. 239).[3]

I shall illustrate what I mean here by describing two studies of aspects of the change from early modern to modern British society. The first is taken from Thomas's exploration of the ways in which humans saw themselves in relation to the 'natural world' of animals and plants that they inhabited (1983). In the three hundred years from 1500 to 1800 these relationships were in a process of transformation. They began with an overwhelming consensus that the natural world was a different order of creation that existed for human exploitation. To think of cruelty in how one used animals was absurd and anachronistic because man inhabited an intrinsically hostile world that had to be continually fought against, subjected and controlled. By the end of the period there were significant trends of change. It would be hard to estimate the extent to which new attitudes had spread throughout English society but amongst influential minorities a new complex of attitudes had largely been established. A complex that has become more powerful and pervasive in the course of the political institutionalisation of modernity.

Thomas summarises the character of these changes under four headings. The first is the shift from a rural to an urban population, begun in earnest in the eighteenth and established irreversibly in the nineteenth century. Partly because of the new density of urban conglomerations and partly because of associated social problems, the countryside became sentimentalised: 'a combination of literary fashion and social factors had created a genuine tension between the relentless progress of urbanisation and the rural longing to which an increasing number of people were subject' (1983, p. 253). The second and clearly related process of change was in attitudes towards distinctions between wilderness and cultivation. The latter is classically a display of civilisation, the order of human society imposed on incoherent nature.

In the later eighteenth century these assumptions were significantly modified by an aesthetic of the picturesque and more generally by the values of romanticism so that the wilderness became seen as a means of access to elemental truths. This in turn leads on to the third characteristic change which was a shift in attitudes away from the pleasures of destructive exploitation of animals and a rejection of dysfunctional aspects of nature towards feelings of responsibility for conservation. In time a concern with preserving an idealised sense of nature would lead in our century to the creation of 'landscape gardens, green belts and animal sanctuaries' (1983, p. 287).

Fundamental to the changing attitudes towards the natural world then is an increasing self-consciousness about the ethics of those relations. It could not be, except for a doctrinaire minority, a simple shift from barbarism to enlightenment but was a more complex process of re-thinking the boundaries of human sociality. This is brought out clearly in the fourth and final characteristic of change which was the growth in those who found eating animals repugnant and, more generally, rejected forms of exploitation which used animals for human entertainment. In particular, the embarrassment about eating meat indicates how a new sensibility was being forged, one in which a cultural conception of identity, privileging ethical and aesthetic values, became an attractive indeed even 'natural' choice for some. The polemical force of this sensibility was not confined to a moment of social transition but has remained politically potent as: 'a growing conflict between the new sensibilities and the material foundations of human society', and thus as Thomas concludes: 'one of the contradictions upon which modern civilisation may be said to rest' (1983, p. 303).

The reason for citing this particular study of changing attitudes is in the idea that amongst particular groups a way of engaging with the cultural order of their environment became invested with significance. A way of engaging that I have referred to as a sensibility. By the term sensibility I mean, in part, a way of responding to events, or actions or phenomena that has a certain pattern or coherence, to the extent that identifying a sensibility provides a way of explaining or predicting responses to new situations. I also mean to indicate that these responses and choices are imbued by those concerned with ethical and aesthetic significance – ways of living that are fundamental to a sense of identity. Most typically, the contemporary exponents of this sensibility spoke of their attitudes as a concern with civilisation as contrasted with the barbarism of those whose attitudes to nature were more traditional.

Other examples of traditional attitudes that were beginning

to be found repugnant come in the moves by reformers to stamp out blood sports (Malcolmson 1973), in particular those sports in which animals were pitched in combat with each other for human entertainment. The same sort of people who found these traditions repugnant also objected to what Spierenburg has called 'the spectacle of suffering' (1984; see also Foucault 1977). Here forms of punishment inscribed upon the body and particularly capital punishment were either abandoned as uncivilised in European countries or moved behind the protective walls of specialised institutions. This new sensibility of civilisation was associated with other social distinctions. In the hundred years between the middle of the eighteenth and the middle of the nineteenth centuries, there was an increasing emphasis on an idealised contrast between the coarse brutalities of the public sphere and the restrained gentility and gendered space of the private home (Davidoff and Hall 1987). In this ideology of domesticity we can begin to see more clearly the emergence of a sensibility that was delineating the contours of a lifestyle.

I said earlier that I would mention two studies of social change. The second is concerned with a period slightly later than the previous one and has a broader cultural remit than the English middle class (Weber 1975). William Weber's study of the emergent taste publics amongst the middle class of modernising societies will, however, further develop the expansion of notions of social structure that I am trying to present. In the era before the establishment of industries of mass entertainment musical concerts provided a European culture of sophisticated taste. Weber argues that the concert world is a relatively modern phenomenon, rapidly expanding in all cities in number and significance in the period between the end of the Napoleonic era and the revolutions of 1848. After that time the concert world was consolidated as one of the principal sources of entertainment for a distinctive social stratum in the structure of a cultural form that has persisted until the end of the twentieth century: 'The turbulent events between 1830 and 1848 brought, then, an independent artistic field such as had never been known in Western music history' (1975, p. 7).

Although distinctive public institutions of the musical concert were established in this era there were several types of concert and, more significantly for our purposes, at least three major musical styles. These were an operatic style emphasising excerpts and selections, which tended to be combined with a related instrumental style emphasising virtuoso skills used to communicate emotional power and passion. In contrast there was a smaller (in terms of size of public and number of concerts) German classical style based upon the works of Haydn, Mozart, Beethoven and Schubert: 'Conflict between the German classical style and its two competitors permeated all concert life during the first half of the century... it amounted to an unusually strong dispute between forms of high culture and popular culture' (Weber 1975, p. 19).

Weber is therefore arguing that, although the new public institution of musical concerts with their associated forms and social rituals were dominated by and displayed the pre-eminence of the new middle classes in national culture, musical taste within this social world was not a unified phenomenon. Indeed, he suggests that there was a broad distinction between the traditional professions within the bourgeoisie and newer, more commercial wealth. Lines of social affiliation were articulated through musical taste so that: 'The people who went to the major kinds of concerts made distinct taste publics. The differences between them stemmed... from a broad division in tastes and life-styles' (1975, p. 22; for an interestingly complementary study of the social organisation of the differentiation of cultural publics see also DiMaggio 1982a and b).

Those involved in propagating new values in the treatment of animals and the natural world, and in using the new institution of concerts to express their feelings of a 'natural' affinity with particular musical styles, would not have spoken of their choices as lifestyle choices. That phrasing would only become possible much later. It is, however, feasible for us to see that the choices made related to new features of modern social conditions – the urbanisation of society and the development of new cultural forms – and displayed cultural affiliations that cut across and made more elaborate the class structure of urban-industrial society. In these respects new forms of social identity were being formulated based upon features that we can identify in the examples I have used, and that subsequently we can see to have been intrinsic to the phenomena of lifestyles.

What I have referred to as the features of new forms of social identity in these instances can be briefly characterised at this stage. The first is conveyed by my use of the term choices. The attitudes, values and tastes that were characteristic of the members of these new social groups were, as I have said, identified by themselves as being significant. In the contemporary public discourse of newspaper articles, sermons, poems, and moralising tracts authors recorded and reflected upon how cultural tastes were imbued with moral seriousness. It became accepted that one's tastes were responsibilities by which you would be judged by others. They were therefore integral to a sense of identity.

The second feature is that these choices were as I have said cultural or, more precisely, focused on those areas of life that were part of leisure or consumption activities. The fuller implications of this point will be considered at greater length in the next chapter, for now the important point is that these areas are themselves distinctive characteristics of modernity. They represent significant aspects of freedoms that had previously been restricted to extremely privileged minorities. Third, however personal the values and tastes were that were being expressed, they fell into distinctive patterns that were themselves associated with other socio-structural characteristics. I have referred to these patterns of affiliation as sensibilities or one could say elective affinities. They seemed to the participants concerned to be consistent with and help to make sense of other aspects of their life-worlds. It is this hard-to-define characteristic of 'natural' association that gives lifestyles an unproblematic sense of order.

Although I have followed a very different route from Sobel in reaching a way of summarising the multiplicity of uses of lifestyle, his proposed definition that a lifestyle is 'any distinctive, and therefore recognizeable, mode of living' (1981, p. 3), can now be seen as uncontroversial. I will add that the mode is usually shared by a reasonable number of people otherwise it shades into idiosyncrasy or eccentricity, and would also accept his emphasis that the way of living primarily consists of 'expressive' behaviours.[4] Sobel goes on to argue that in the history of the United States such expressive behaviour has come to be focused on consuming goods and services. This leads to a further suggestion that lifestyles can be seen as functional responses to modernity. In particular as new means of integration in the anomic worlds of suburbia, and as responses to the secularisation, and consequent loss of meaning, of everyday life. Both of these functional themes have been widely used in different ways to explain the cultural changes of modernity and will recur throughout the book.

We can then begin to see some of the ways in which lifestyles, as patterns of action and as a distinct type of social grouping, are embedded in the social order of modernity. They work as a set of expectations which act as a form of ordered control on the emerging social uncertainties of mass society. These expectations are not of course mandatory or obligatory, although individuals may experience them as such, but patterns of ways of living that flesh out the general contours of class structured distinction (see for example the studies of leisure lifestyles and several forms of stratified disadvantage in Henry 1994, Pt. 3).

Lifestyles are, precisely because of the features I have just tried to describe, intrinsically members' categories. This does not mean that they exist at a high level of theoretical specification but that people use lifestyles in everyday life to identify and explain wider complexes of identity and affiliation. They are part of the practical vocabularies of everyday life: 'life-styles are artificial creations or adoptions. The bearer himself is aware of the fact that the style can be donned and discarded at will and, therefore, it can be acted out with some degree of self-irony and self-satire' (Bensman and Vidich 1995, p. 239).[5] In sum, lifestyles are interpretive resources – forms of local knowledge[6] that are necessarily approximate but nonetheless significant in the politics of mass society.

NOTES

1 Kafka is a poet of modernity who in his novels was able to evoke all too clearly a citizen's sense of helplessness at the operation of bureaucratic power over which they have no control.

2 In general I am using structure here in the spirit of Giddens's theory of structuration – as resources that enable as well as constrain (Giddens 1993).

3 Although Zablocki and Kanter (1976) have suggested that there are two types of lifestyle – one based on more traditional criteria of stratification and a more recent alternative which has developed from certain groups' rejection of traditional values – they also emphasise differences of choice within a rough equality of opportunity.

4 Zablocki and Kanter similarly suggest that a lifestyle might be defined: 'to the extent that the members are similar to one another and different from others both in the distribution of disposable incomes and the motivations that underlie such distributions' (1976, p. 270).

5 See also Bocock: 'Modern consumers are physically passive, but mentally they are very busy. Consumption is more than ever before an experience which is to be located in the head,

a matter of the brain and the mind, rather than seen as the process of simply satisfying biological needs' (1993, p. 51).

6 I am using local knowledge to refer to forms of life shared within cultural or geographic localities – a usage I develop more fully in the third part of the book.

2

Consumer culture

In the first chapter I argued that lifestyles are a distinctively modern form of status grouping. The modernity of this type of association lies, in part, in the way that the status, conferred by membership of the group, does not stem exclusively from the occupations that members of the group share or even from the privileges they are commonly able to enjoy; but rather from how they use those privileges and resources that they are able to enjoy. Lifestyles are therefore usually assumed to be based upon the social organisation of consumption, and I stress associated normative outlooks, rather than the social organisation of production which has classically been taken to be the basis of class structures.

Consumption is used throughout the book in its broadest sense to refer to all the types of social activity that people do that we might use to characterise and identify them, other than (or in addition to) what they might 'do' for a living. Although even this is questionable as the clarity of a distinction between work and non-work activities is very hard to sustain. It seems that part of the shift away from seeing productive status as the basis of social identity is that increasing numbers of people choose their type of work and how it is organised in order to be consistent with lifestyle values (see for example Olszewska and Roberts 1989). I should also note that consumption has a broader compass than social structures of production. For one thing it includes all those who do not work, such as the young, the old and the unemployed, as well as, most significantly, women who in modern economies have not typically been expected to be economic producers.

Consumption as it is conceived here therefore necessarily includes the social patterns of leisure which I shall characterise as new expectations for the control and use of time in personally meaningful ways. Bocock is right to insist that 'consumption is a socially constructed, historically changing process' (1993, p. 45). The idea that consumption has become (or is becoming) both a central focus of social life and cultural values underlies a more general notion of consumer culture. In this chapter I will discuss the constitutive significance of consumer culture and a leisure economy for modernity and the social affiliations of lifestyles. Although Bocock is also right to go on to make a distinction between the era of mass consumption – which he dates from the 1950s onwards – and preceding developments, I will argue in this section that important themes in the development of consumerism help to elucidate the character of a mass consumer culture.

The social changes in early-modern Europe were clearly dependent upon, and displayed in, a number of concurrent changes such as the development of international markets, the growth in a trade in art objects and luxury goods, and the growth of new urban social classes replacing a feudal social structure (see for example Schama 1987, especially Part 2). These changes stimulated new modes of production and were inseparable from the disintegration of a continental religious culture into new state economies, but were also dependent upon the development of attitudes positively valuing fashionable goods, household furnishings and new modes of inquiry and topics for discussion (Mukerji 1983; Weatherill 1988). It is in these attitudes that we can see the growth of the voracious imagination that is another dimension of consumer culture. The fuller flowering of this imagination though was dependent upon the establishment of an urban public culture oriented to the marketing of fashion (McKendrick *et al.* 1983; Brewer and Porter 1992).

McKendrick writes of eighteenth-century England as witnessing the birth of a consumer society and facilitating a consumer revolution, in the process overcoming barriers that 'required

changes in attitude and thought, changes in prosperity and standards of living, changes in commercial technique and promotional
skills, sometimes even changes in the law itself' (1983, p. 2). If one
asks why England set a precedent in this revolution, a central
element in McKendrick's answer would be the relatively narrow
spread of the contemporary social structure. The new manufac-
turers of consumer goods did initially target elite audiences, and
their endorsement was essential for the creation of popular
fashion, but massive profits were made by subsequently distributing and marketing versions of these goods for anonymous audiences. In the process the rigid distinctions of caste society, in
appearance and life-world which had been protected by the conservatism of the sumptuary laws amongst other factors, were
necessarily robbed of their clarity. In the process of creating
anonymous audiences through the commercialisation of fashion,
advertising and other marketing techniques were centrally
important.

Thus McKendrick mentions new methods of display, the
manipulation of fashion through artificial obsolescence, the development of new places and agents of sale and 'how the manipulation of social emulation made men pursue "luxuries" where they
had previously bought "decencies", and "decencies" where they
had previously bought "necessities" ' (1983, p. 98). Central to the
luxuries of the previously privileged elites that the new middle
classes had begun to see as appropriate to themselves was the
luxury of leisure and the pleasure of entertainments with which
to fill it.[1] The communal play and celebrations of early modern
Europe (see Burke 1978) were gradually superseded by the commercial provision of drama, music, dancing and sports, etc. And
most notably by the development of leisure towns or tourist resorts
such as the spas of eighteenth-century England: 'In the early
eighteenth century, culture and sport slowly ceased to be élitist and
private and became increasingly public' (Plumb in McKendrick *et
al.* 1983, p. 284); a process of the commercialisation of leisure
which continued to grow in the nineteenth century. I think it
is significant for the subsequent emphasis upon domesticity in
consumer advertising that Plumb picks out the commercialisation
of children as new luxury or leisure objects for parental indulgence
as an essential part of the emergent consumer culture.[2]

It has been conventional to emphasise the rationalism of the
emergent public sphere of the eighteenth century, focused on a
discourse of politics, trade and culture. There has consequently

been a neglect of the extent to which this discourse was dependent from the beginning on the raucous vulgarity of rampant commercialism. Re-thinking the dynamics of modernisation involves moving away from a view in which it is primarily emphasised that modernity involves 'the replacement of the Providence-dominated world of early modern and medieval Europe by the world of expanding knowledge and science, of discoverable nature and rational exploration' (Plumb in McKendrick *et al.* 1983, p. 333), towards a greater stress on hedonism and a search for personal meaningfulness. In this respect the role of romanticism in Campbell's (1987) account of the impetus of consumer culture introduces a necessary utopian strain. The hedonism of modern consumerism, it is argued, is to be understood as a search for the interdependence of pleasure and meaning in the endlessly renewing temptations that the market makes available. The logic of modernity is that fashion is not irrational exploitation but an existential search for distinction in a deeply secular culture.[3]

I have attempted to show that consumerism has been central to the social development of modernity. It is, however, clear that a consumer culture has been a more recent innovation. The force of the idea of a consumer culture is dependent upon the possibility of mass marketing with its concomitant mass advertising. Before turning to look more directly at how notions of lifestyles have been used in this century, it is relevant to look in slightly greater detail at themes that can be picked out from studies of the institutionalisation of mass marketing. It is unsurprising that the greater part of the literature on the history of consumerism is concerned with the era covering the last quarter of the nineteenth century and the first decades of the twentieth. It was during this period that the indiscriminate availability of standardised goods across national markets that is the prerequisite of a full consumer culture was established (Fraser 1981; Strasser 1989). It was in this era then that the basic cultural themes of the mass societies of the twentieth century were established – in particular a willingness by ordinary people to invest resources in the pursuit of style.[4]

Amongst these basic cultural themes is the transformation of 'natural' order. I noted above that consumer marketing in the eighteenth century had to override established status distinctions and thus shrink social differences. Complementing and intensifying the same process, mass marketing at the end of the nineteenth century 'shrank' the hinterland from which supplies could be taken. The development of fast, efficient rail networks in addition to improved sea and road transport not only meant that far-flung places could be brought into metropolitan markets, but that those markets could draw supplies nationally and internationally conquering time, space and the natural order (Schivelbusch 1980).

We are led by this theme to emphasise the artificiality of this culture, an artificiality that was enhanced by a dramaturgy of spectacular display. The 'market' of consumer society is an abstract entity transcending the specific markets of small retailers. The physically bounded spaces of interpersonal markets, with their necessarily accompanying dramas of social interaction, are transformed in the transitions to modernity (Slater 1993). These new markets exist as potential incorporating a huge terrain and innumerable sites (a process of abstraction that was enhanced from its beginnings by schemes of extended payment and developed more recently by the introduction of 'plastic money' and other forms of credit transactions).

The abstract potential of consumer indulgence was given form by the development of city centres as places of exaggerated entertainment – the fantasy of eighteenth-century pleasure gardens made over into a more elaborate world of illusion (Barth 1980). The introduction of electric light and public transport systems meant that traditional boundaries of day and night could be superseded (Schivelbusch 1988). And the crowds of customers thus attracted were entertained by a whole variety of new eating places, by dazzling and luxurious bars and saloons, by elaborate theatres and the earliest cinemas soon to be known as dream palaces and by new forms of display using the facilities of plate glass windows, electric lighting, steel and brick construction and all the resources of architectural spectacle to transform public space (Bronner 1989; Williams 1982).[5]

Above all, the new era of consumer culture was inaugurated and institutionalised in the rise of department stores (Chaney 1983; Laermans 1993; Lancaster 1994). These palaces of endless profusion of goods offered new freedoms and new opportunities for indulgence. Shopping was transformed from the provision of necessities or the personal negotiation of new acquisitions. In the impersonal anonymity of utopian display shoppers were all free to wander as and how they wished and to use the endless facilities to seek out personal tastes and construct personal itineraries (for the first time, as Rob Shields has christened a collection of essays (1992), 'lifestyle shopping' became both possible and standard). In addition, however, to opening up new opportunities for urban masses, the department stores required new social disciplines. Much as in the way that the self-service garage nearly a hundred years later requires customers to learn new responsibilities and mutual consideration, so the department store encapsulated new forms of crowd discipline and respectful disattention.

I have suggested that the department stores were a very visible element in the transformation of metropolitan centres, offering new opportunities to anonymous customers – both in person and by mail – to ransack the goods of the world. (It should be clear that although the promise of equal access was undoubtedly present in new forms of retailing, this did not mean that prior inequalities of resource were in any way lessened.) More generally, the stores were also part of a metropolitan hubris in which through the dreams of an imperialist imagination, the world outside modernity was being made available for exploitation. A number of writers have pointed to the diet of exhibitions, fairs, centennials, expositions, etc. which were held in all European capitals and many European and North American cities in the century between 1850 and 1950 as extending the ideology of consumerism into political, cultural and technological stages (de Cauter 1993; Greenhalgh 1988; Ley and Olds 1988). In part these jamborees served to boost local products, initiatives and culture, but they were also part of a wider imperialist agenda in which the intrinsic benefits of civilisation could be equated with the forms of life of new urban masses (Pred 1994).

I have tried to show how the new social form of lifestyles was coloured by some of the broader narratives of the cultural forms of consumerism. These can be summarised briefly under the headings of: fantasy; excess; spectacle; and citizenship. While the first three are I hope reasonably self-evident from what has been said already, the last is I assume a more puzzling term. I use it because I can find no good way of summarising the idea that mass marketing, as with other forms of mass democracy, offers the illusions of equal participation, and indeed even the glory of national culture, without much of its substantive powers. In combination these narratives amplify and develop what I have called above the artificiality of mass marketing. In so doing they can easily be taken over by the several forms of critical theories of consumerism – theories which stress the incitement of false needs, the illusions of satisfaction and the propagation of inauthentic values (a powerful version based in the Marxist tradition of this critique is Haug 1986; see also Cross 1993).

I think the moral critique of consumerism as introducing 'inauthentic' cravings or needs (what Bocock (1993) sees as the alienation inherent in the stimulation of desire) is misplaced because it presupposes an original or essential way of being-in-the-world that shuns adornments and the dramaturgy of display. At the same time I recognise that there is a necessary and much wider cultural ambivalence about the social changes of consumerism (Bronner 1989; Fox and Jackson Lears 1983; Horowitz 1985). I have tried to indicate the existence of ethical and aesthetic, at best, ambivalence over the implications of consumerism by emphasising that as lifestyles display normative sensibilities then they will express quite contrasting responses to the values of consumerism. An ambivalence of approach that has most clearly underlain a general disparagement, both intellectually and popularly, of the social implications of mass advertising (Ewen 1976; Ewen and Ewen 1982; Marchand 1985). Again, one cannot summarise a complex history with a brief judgement on the validity of a cultural form, but it is obvious that the mass marketing of consumer culture could not have been institutionalised without the rhetorical forms of mass advertising (Schudson 1993).

I rather suspect that some of the driving force in critiques of consumerism has stemmed from a moral paternalism that fears that women are particularly vulnerable to irrational persuasion. The assumption that women are the primary customers of consumer culture has probably become outmoded in recent years but was traditionally grounded in the distinctions between production and consumption. With the institutionalisation of public and private spheres that I have referred to in passing earlier, the public sphere was generally understood as a world of work, public matters and men's concerns with organisational matters. In contrast, the private sphere was focused on the home, family relationships and women's concerns with servicing both the family lifestyle and other family members (Hall 1992). The distinction between the spheres was physically inscribed in the differences between home and work, a distinction that became even clearer with the development of suburban housing with a clear separation between occupational and residential sectors. The progress of suburban development cannot be treated in any detail here (Fishman 1987; Jackson 1985), but is central to the development of consumer culture in two ways.

The first has been indicated in what I have said about the development of city centres as spectacular sites of display and entertainment. These centres, and their minor echoes in satellite and provincial towns, were surrounded by and acted as a focus for the anonymous ranks of suburban housing. The city centre in its role as spectacular centre for visiors from the suburbs provided a new form of public space increasingly accessible to respectable women. In particular, department stores depended upon their female customers and were increasingly staffed by female assistants. On the other side, the increasing importance of the suburban home as the centre of family life was recognised in emotional and financial investment. The home-makers of the suburbs needed the facilities of shops and stores to provide a variety of cheap furnishings and clothes with which to meet the swirling demands of fashion. As leisure time was also increasingly focused on home-based activities there were further opportunities for new clothes and equipment that again stimulated the demand for consumer goods (on British middle-class lifestyle in the first half of the twentieth century see Jackson 1991).

There was therefore a symbiotic relationship between the feminine character of the suburbs and the feminine emphases of consumerism. A complementary interdependence that was also expressed in a second aspect of the development of consumer culture. This takes up the notion of citizenship that I introduced earlier. Suburban housing is the perfect physical form for the citizens of mass consumerism. Virtually indistinguishable and anonymous suburban houses are depressingly normal, but they lack the collectivist character of public housing blocks. Individually distinct, or semi-detached, they encourage private investment in the pursuit of distinction while virtually guaranteeing the impossibility of gross transgression (Bell 1958). With their easy access to the spectacular sites of consumer entertainment they fulfill the promise of democratic access while at the same time reinforcing a series of myths about the dangers of urban congestion in contrast to the privacy of the suburban home.

I have been concerned to show some of the implications of saying that our notions of lifestyle have been developed in, and I think we can say have been dependent on, the context of consumer culture. This close association has not meant, however, that there is no variety in lifestyle practice. I pointed out earlier that consumer marketing was often primarily directed at female customers and yet it would not be true to say that women have been or are now in the vanguard of lifestyle innovation. In the third part of the book I mention at several points how there seem to be gendered differences in lifestyles within a shared social stratum. This both tells us to look for variations in lifestyles as forms of life, and to beware of assuming that lifestyles are extreme displays of consumer infatutation. There are, even so, ideological continuities in consumerism that are reflected in lifestyle discourse.

First, as I have emphasised, is a glorying in the artificiality of marketing. Natural and traditional social constraints on trade are disregarded in flattering the individual customer. This in turn leads to a second quality of spectacular show both of the process of marketing and of individual lifestyles as forms of display. There is also a third quality in which the customer is assumed to be appropriative – things can be taken over and used almost as of right. And this in turn illuminates a fourth quality of a freedom of choice that is simultaneously dependent on the provisions of others. This further leads to a privatisation of pleasure in which goods and services and experiences are acquired individually even if used to impress a community. This is a brief and necessarily elliptical review of an ideological climate. The interdependence between these themes and changing forms of social order will be brought out more clearly in the discussion of relevant social theorists in the next part of the book.

I have so far concentrated on the characteristics of the emergent consumer culture. I have therefore neglected the concomitant development of leisure industries except in as much as leisure is one of the goods of a flourishing consumer culture. I mentioned earlier that the commercialisation of leisure, that is a shift from communal forms of play and celebration to commercial forms of entertainment supplied by entrepreneurs, was an essential step in the development of a distinctive middle-class culture. It was inevitable that new commercial ventures in entertainment would be primarily directed at middle-class audiences as they had the resources to find the time and money for these entertainments. And of course the entertainments that were institutionalised as cultural forms, such as the world of concerts we have already mentioned or the development of a respectable theatre later in the nineteenth century, marked out the establishment of a distinctive class culture. Even so, it is also important to recognise that the worlds of the new urban-industrial working class were also given a distinctive character by the provision of commercial leisure from the beginning (Cunningham 1980; Walvin 1978).

One of the most direct indicators of the growth of new markets for leisure is the rapid increase in size of British coastal towns and certain spas (the latter more commonly in continental Europe) acting as holiday resorts over the last two hundred years. While these resorts were quickly stratified by social class, in terms of their ambience and types of entertainment offered as well as the average cost of staying there, they did collectively show the existence of a mass market for a time away from normality which has burgeoned into the tourist industry of the twentieth century (Rojek 1993). Similarly, although the mixture of shopping opportunities and leisure facilities in city centres was initially directed primarily at a middle-class clientele, with the development of cinema films as the first mass medium of popular entertainment new cultural forms of mass leisure quickly colonised the language of the leisure industries (Chanan 1980; May 1980; Sklar 1978). None of these processes was of course ideologically neutral. The extension of mass leisure was not just a process of rising living standards and shortening working hours; it was also a deliberate drive towards reducing class conflict and minimising differences between class cultures (Bailey 1978; Clarke and Critcher 1985).

The social and cultural history of the development of leisure investment in the twentieth century has largely been the inauguration of new industries of mass entertainment. In addition to the cinema already mentioned, one would point here to mass publishing, the rise of radio and television industries and associated forms of entertainment such as popular photography, video recordings and popular music recordings. More recently the development of electronic games to be played either in arcades or on machines at home has been another example of high capital investment in leisure facilities. These leisure industries are clearly significant for any account of lifestyles not only because they occupy such a large part of their audiences' leisure time, but also because they employ large numbers of people in production and presentation and they require large capital investment to sustain their market. Leisure industries are therefore analogous to other forms of consumer goods in that they display the same structural characteristic we noted earlier of metropolitan standardised provision being complemented by privatised, often domestic, consumption.

Responses earlier this century to the development of mass culture were largely pessimistic on the grounds that it would either undermine standards of high culture and/or that we would all end up looking at, listening to, or reading the same diet. I suppose one way of understanding the function of a category of lifestyles is that these fears, at least in the latter respect, have proved unfounded. The negotiation and use of facilities provided by consumption and leisure industries by mass audiences has proved considerably more complex than the elitist fears of earlier cultural commentators allowed. This is not to say, as I have emphasised, that the meaning of lifestyle choices is necessarily complex or authentic. But I have tried to show that conventional expectations of these choices cannot be understood without being placed in the social and cultural history of the development of the modern world. We can now go on to look in greater detail in the next chapter at some aspects of how a language of lifestyles has been used in more recent years.

NOTES

1 I have discussed several of the themes reviewed in this chapter at greater length although from a very different perspective in Chaney (1993), Chapter 5.
2 It is also worth noting that the birth of the consumer society was also the time when household pets became sentimentalised and objects of indulgent spending by their owners.
3 It is important in this respect to remember that the first time fashion was given ideological significance was in revolutionary France at the end of the eighteenth century (Hunt 1984).
4 Liebergott, for example, has noted that between 1900 and 1929 US Navy expenditures on clothing personnel rose by 16 per cent due to rising wages and material costs, but that during the same period average civilian expenditure on clothing by males increased 150 per cent and by females by 492 per cent (1993, p. 93).
5 On contemporary literary responses to cultural change see Bowlby (1985), and more generally on changes in the public space of nineteenth-century cities see Sennett (1977, especially Part 2).

3

Lifestyle uses

In a paper reviewing theories of consumer culture (reprinted as Chapter 2 in 1991), Featherstone identifies three types. The first looks at consumerism as a particular mode or stage of capitalist development. The second is a more sociological concern with the relationships between the use of goods and ways of delineating status: 'The focus here is upon the different ways in which people use goods in order to create social bonds or distinctions' (1991, p. 13). And third, there are those who are concerned with the creativity of consumer practices – the aesthetics of consumption. I will take up this third approach in the last part of this book. For this chapter, I assume that the ways of using that are mentioned in the second of Featherstone's types are in effect lifestyles. I will therefore discuss some instances of how lifestyles as networks of inclusion and differentiation have been used in social analysis.

It is because these social networks are concerned with the use of goods, the majority of which can be packaged and marketed so that they can be sold, that their empirical study is particularly important for marketing organisations. Here research is clearly functional, undertaken in order to generate a particular type of knowledge. The contours of what I have called networks or lifestyles are in this perspective a type of social map. They enable us to lay out the topography of different sorts of audiences for products. Research which generates data that can be used to chart character-istic lifestyles can take the theoretical and historical preliminaries explored previously for granted. It can be assumed to be a straight-forward matter of investigating people's habits and attitudes in order to see how lifestyles as markets are likely to develop in the future.

Market research organisations such as Mintel aim to provide information that is relevant to understanding spending habits in Britain and other European markets. In a special report on British lifestyles (Mintel 1988) 'The primary purpose ... is to track ten year spend trends of households' (p. 3), as well as including more specific sections on aspects of the lifestyles of the young and women and some data on women as decision makers. As an indication of the sorts of heads that are thought likely to be particularly useful, I shall list the twelve sections into which the report is divided: the people; where the money comes from; where the money goes; spending on the home and its contents; spending on food, drink and tobacco products; spending on holidays and entertainment; spending on the person, mobility, health and edu-cation; spending on insurance, pensions, savings and tax; the young adult and lifestyle; women and lifestyle; married women as finan-cial decision makers (in this section is provided 'the very latest research insight into the degree to which women are involved in decision making over financial matters' (1988, p. 4)); and British attitudes to Europe (see also Mintel 1994).

More specifically, I shall report some aspects of the data pre-sented in the chapter in the 1988 report on young adults and lifestyle variables, noting particularly factors of gendered differ-ence and change. If young adulthood is the period between child-hood and the assumption of full adult responsibilities, the period divided here into two age groups of 15–19 year olds and 20–24 year olds, then it seems that contemporary British young adults wish to extend the 'freedoms' of the period for as long as possible. Both men and women are delaying the age of first marriage to a mean of 24.6 for women and 26.9 for men. And although the number of women in their early twenties cohabiting is increasing, and conceptions out of wedlock are less likely to lead to marriage, the number of live births per thousand for young women aged 20–24 has fallen from 172.6 in 1961 to 83.4 in 1987. Complementing these trends there are clear indications that the numbers of young people staying in full-time education after 16 is increasing for both sexes but particularly markedly amongst young women (although high rates of youth unemployment in the 1980s must be borne in mind in this respect).

It seems then that the period of being young (with its implied individual autonomy) is lasting longer and offering more equal opportunities to both sexes. Although it should be noted that while young men and women in employment start off at equal gross weekly earnings, a clear difference has already emerged amongst the 20–24 year old group[1] – a difference that is probably related to the preponderance of those young women who are in work in secretarial, clerical and shop assisting jobs. Turning to spending priorities, differences in gendered styles are clearly apparent (Table 3.1; there is also a reference to class differences in rank-ordering of priorities but this is not tabulated).

Table 3.1 Spending priorities of young adults, 1988 (Base: 1138 – percentages)

	All young adults	Men	Women
Clothes	63	40	79
Music	36	44	27
Going out/drinking	26	34	19
Personal appearance	16	3	30
Savings	14	11	16
Books	8	7	10
Hobbies	8	12	3
Sport	8	14	2
Vehicles	7	12	3

Source: BMRB/Mintel (Mintel 1988, p. 9.8)

Table 3.2 Elements in life which matter most to young adults, 1988 (Base: 1138 – percentages)

	Men	Women
Relationship with family	57	80
Relationships with opposite sex	38	38
Relationships with own age group	31	37
Going out and having a good time	37	27
Freedom and independence	31	31
Work or study satisfaction	27	27
Hobbies and sports	26	13
Spending money on oneself	14	11

Source: BMRB/Mintel (Mintel 1988, p. 9.15)

In subsequent tables a pattern of gendered spheres becomes clearer and more pronounced with increasing age. For example participating in some form of sport falls sharply for all youths in their twenties but particularly strongly amongst young women as soon as they start cohabiting or they get married. Similarly the frequency with which women go out in the evening falls markedly with age and with marriage and family responsibilities. It is also clear that there are strong gendered differences amongst young adults when asked what elements in life mattered most to them (Table 3.2).

I have clearly not tried to present a review of young adults' lifestyles then, but rather indicate the sorts of trends that lifestyle analysis by marketing organisations identifies.[2] Pursued in greater detail these trends segment the market by what Michman sees as cultural influences rather than personality traits (1991). Seizing on a constellation of variables the social analyst is able to characterise different segments of the market in ways that illuminate their receptiveness to different types of product development or marketing strategy. For example, Michman cites a study of newspaper readers in Florida that divided them into twelve groups (percentage market share in brackets after each group): Young, bored and blue (12); Tomorrow's leaders (3); Achievers (5); Mr Middle (18): Senior solid conservatives (7); Winter affluents (2); Ms Restless (3); Expanded outlook (2); Mid-life optimists (21); Domestic inactives (10); Nostalgics (5); Mrs Senior Traditionalist (12) (1991, pp. 1–3). Michman does not comment on what a profoundly depressing profile this must be for Florida publishers, but for us it serves to illustrate the evocative labelling of lifestyles.[3]

I do not expand upon the category headings for Florida newspaper readers as I hope they are sufficiently clear. What is more important about them than their specific referents in that study, is that they denote 'outlooks' that are more wide-ranging than their expectations of newspapers. By outlooks here I mean a cluster of values concerning politics and ethics as well as a multi-faceted social style. I can explain what I mean by referring to another section when Michman discusses changing gender roles. He cites a study reporting that '80% of young husbands participate in the care of children under 12, 53% wash dishes, 47% cook for the family, 39% vacuum the house, 32% shop for food, 29% do some of the laundry, and 28% sometimes clean the bathroom' (1991, p. 191). One can of course deplore the inequalities still displayed in these figures (and suspect the extent to which they are optimistic reports), but the point Michman emphasises to those responsible for marketing strategies is that male lifestyles are changing. In catering to these changing sensibilities suppliers of consumer goods and services need to be sensitive to the symbolic meanings of their products.

The inferences to be drawn from the way a notion of lifestyles is being used in these marketing perspectives are two-fold. First, that lifestyle analysis cannot be a static categorisation but must focus on social trends in both structural as well as attitudinal variables; and, second, that analysis must focus on the cultural implications of social trends: 'In finer and finer detail social scientists, advertisers and market researchers have differentiated consumption behaviors into "lifestyle" categories and in so doing have assisted the development of increasingly specific frameworks for both product distribution and political expression' (O'Brien 1995, p. 197, who also surveys some illustrative research).

In what seems to me to be the most substantial chapter of his book, Michman summarises the data of a large number of studies in America to produce five emergent lifestyle trends for the post-1980s. These are, first, what he calls a trend towards voluntary simplicity: 'Consumers who adopt this lifestyle seek material simplicity, strive for self-realisation, purchase do-it-yourself products, and adapt an ecological ethic' (1991, p. 147). He estimates that a quarter of the American market may subscribe to these values with many more adopting certain elements. This latter, larger, group of sympathisers can be partly characterised by two further trends of those a) seeking self-fulfilment through 'Purchasing goods and services that are meaningful to them rather than symbols of conspicuous consumption' (1991, p. 146); and b) with lowered expectations of standards of living. Finally, the two remaining trends are of an increasing lack of time, particularly amongst women as more now work full time, and of maturing tastes with an ageing population.[4]

Such lifestyle trends are of course contentious propositions and it is not my purpose now to attempt to assess their empirical validity. It is relevant in relation to this to remind ourselves from a British government sponsored review of social trends (Central Statistical Office (hereafter CSO) 1994) how much more lifestyle variables are stratified by social class (generally on British social change this century see Johnson 1994). So that, if, for example, we tabulate the percentage of adults with no natural teeth by age and socio-economic group in 1991 we find a very clear correlation between lack of teeth and lower occupational status (Table 3.3).

It seems likely that differences in diet, in part as a function of cultural differences in attitudes towards the body, will be a factor in such findings. Therefore a general report on changing diets towards 'healthier' lifestyles – such as 'In 1992 each person ate, on average, under five ounces of beef and veal per week, only about half the amount consumed in 1961 ... [while] ... Lamb and mutton consumption has fallen more sharply' (CSO 1994, p. 98) – has to be put in context. Another table, relating heavy cigarette smoking and consumption of alcohol above what is depressingly called sensible limits to socio-economic group in 1990 (Table 3.4), shows clear correlations between smoking and lower occupational status amongst males and females, but almost no difference on alcohol consumption amongst males and an inverse correlation amongst females.

Table 3.3 Percentage of adults with no natural teeth by age and socio-economic group, 1991

	16–44	*45–64*	*65+*
Professional	1	5	28
Employers and managers	1	10	42
Intermediate and junior non-manual	2	15	49
Skilled and semi-skilled manual	6	55	67
Unskilled manual	6	38	78

Source: General Household Survey (CSO 1994, p. 98)

Table 3.4 Heavy cigarette smoking (>20 per day) and alcohol consumption (>22 units for males and >15 units for females per week) by socio-economic group 1990 (percentages)

	Males		*Females*	
	Smoking	*Alcohol*	*Smoking*	*Alcohol*
Professional	5	26	6	14
Employers and managers	12	30	7	14
Intermediate and junior non-manual	8		7	
		26		11
Skilled manual	17	28	11	9
Semi-skilled manual	18	26	12	9
Unskilled manual	22	26	13	6

Source: General Household Survey (CSO 1994, p. 99)

Using lifestyles to segment, or as I would prefer to say map, markets is then more complex than merely collecting data on habits and preferences. Not only does the analyst need to know the context of changes in diet, or leisure habits or expectations for gender roles, they also need to know the cultural significance of different types of change. In the same way that audiences are not static social categories, lifestyles are forms of collective identity that develop through time – even in what often seems a defiant novelty they may implicitly refer to aspects of collective memory.[5] I have introduced a reference to audiences because audience research has come up against many of the issues that we can now see confronting lifestyle analysis. An audience may seem to be a group that is in some sense attending a performance, and with thus a clear category divide between them and those who are not attending. But of course audiences 'attend' in different ways and to different degrees and the boundaries between membership and not are fluid and impermanent (on audience research see Morley 1992[6]).

I have suggested previously (co-written with Judith Chaney 1979) that audiences can be differentiated internally as well as externally by the use of four variables. The first is nature of access – those who have to actively seek out performances with some difficulty will have different expectations from those to whom something is ubiquitously at hand. The second variable of conception refers to the categorisations that different audiences use in relation to goods and performances, while the third variable of involvement is concerned with the effect of the differential import-ance that audience membership has for constituent groups.[7] Finally, the fourth variable of reward looks to the differences in the sorts of pleasures that activities can generate. In combination they mean that to refer as we might to 'the' audience for *Coronation Street* is only ever a statistical abstraction. There are a number of ways (or styles of attention) through which *Coronation Street* is meaningful and those using these ways are in effect inter-pretive communities (Radway 1987[8]).

To find that the pragmatism of market research using lifestyles quickly leads to talk of interpretive communities suggests that my initial language of sensibilities was not misplaced (see also the study reported in Lunt and Livingstone 1992). Marketing is, how-ever, still necessarily concerned with how lifestyles can be exploited for competitive advantage. This holds true even when one takes account of the sophisticated sponsorship strategies

Schreiber recommends (1994). He describes the development of what he calls event marketing – the use of sponsorship of non-commercial events by companies in order to seem to chime with lifestyle values by target audiences. Thus he cites instances as diverse as Coca-Cola's sponsorship of the Hands Across America demonstration against poverty, Reebok's association with Amnesty International and the desire of companies to be associated with the Olympics, etc.

The reasons Schreiber offers for the success of this rather diffuse, non-directional advertising are four-fold: there are now so many communication media that any appeal is necessarily fragmented; that with a profusion of goods customers have very little brand loyalty; that in many market sectors products are functionally indistinguishable; and that products may be invested with symbolic significance by consumers. If, by sponsoring an altruistic or cultural event or campaign, a company can position themselves as sympathetic to significant values then lifestyle campaigns are 'strategic mainstream marketing that ideally enables the company to ask each consumer whether he or she now feels differently about the company that sponsored the program' (1994, p. 19). The crucial shift in perspective is for companies to appreciate that what Schreiber calls the social value of products or services has replaced (or is replacing) dollar value.

This understanding of lifestyle marketing is closer to a language of sensibilities in that products are imbued with symbolic or social value through being positioned as being implicitly consistent with other lifestyle values. Personal lifestyles in this view generate demands through individuals seeking out goods, services or activities that form a perceived pattern of associations. This should mean that from a certain knowledge of lifestyle factors, researchers could hope to be able to hypothesise other associated factors. I can turn for illustration to the two survey reports by Cox and his associates (1987 and 1993) on patterns of association between health measures and lifestyle factors. The original sample was surveyed in 1984–5 and as many as could be traced were followed up again in 1991–2. In addition to measures of physical and psychological health, both self-judged and technically evaluated, a number of 'lifestyle factors' such as dietary habits, smoking patterns, alcohol consumption and changes in exercise and leisure activities were charted.

In a separate study Blaxter (1990) has used the same four lifestyle variables in conjunction with measures of respondents' social circumstances to chart patterns in health expectations. In Blaxter's work it is clearer that these criteria of lifestyle difference are assumed to be in some degree areas of voluntary choice. In contrast, socio-economic circumstances are recognised to be involuntary constraints. This distinction has generated a debate over whether interventionist policies concerned with social inequalities of health should be aimed at individuals and attempt to change their behaviour, or take a more collective form and address the contexts of individual behaviour. In itself, any explanation of differences in health, and implied concepts of good and bad health, is not our concern here – except that the idea that lifestyles encapsulate attitudes and orientations underlying different types of 'risk' of ill-health has clearly generated a great deal of social policy and health promotion research.

It is relevant to this type of discourse that Blaxter is led to emphasise that 'healthy behaviour' is rarely homogeneous. By this she means that different social groups seem to combine 'good' or 'bad' behaviours in different ways (1990, Chapter 6). While this may seem to the lay person to be a discovery of the obvious, its significance is that the meaning of the same lifestyle variables – such as exercise or social drinking – varies in different social milieux. Researchers concerned with the social distributions of health and healthy practices have therefore to consider attitudes and expectations towards the legitimacy of possible health-inducing actions, as well as measures of behaviour, in order to assess the cumulative stratification of behaviour and circumstance. It seems that, while it is true that 'those who have positive attitudes or believe that behaviour is important are more likely to have "healthy" lifestyles' (1990, p. 181), it is too simple to say that attitudes cause behaviour. Thus when social circumstances such as income and education are held constant the relationships between expectations and actions become more complicated. Lifestyles quickly become rather confused intervening variables between health and the social order.

It seems to me likely that the difficulties which this lifestyle research has generated stem from a conceptualisation of lifestyle variables as each relating to a dimension with a range from positive to negative health implications. In this way 'bad' lifestyle habits function much as other disease inducing agents. An alternative which has recently been gaining ground is to reject health and disease as opposites, in which the one is the positive absence of the other, and rather to see 'health as a resource for everyday life, not merely the objective of living' (Kelly *et al.* 1993, pp. 162–3). O'Brien has pointed out that 'The extension of health into the area of wellbeing can be understood as a process of de-differentiation (or "opening up") of health in the context of everyday life' (1995, p. 195), and in his use of the concept of de-differentiation I suspect deliberately echoes Lash's use of this concept as a characteristic of postmodern experience (1990). It is not therefore surprising that Kelly and his associates characterise this alternative approach as postmodern and suggest it offers a vision of health privileging aesthetic and moral considerations: 'In the postmodern condition, aesthetic considerations are, whether we like it or not, paramount in determining how we choose to lead or shape our own lives and how we assess what is a good life' (1993, p. 163).

To change the style of health research from being a concern with specific problems to a more diffuse concern with 'wellness' involves shifts in the use of related concepts of lifestyle. Such as from acting as a quasi-structural determinant of social action, to being the basis of a search for what seems relevant knowledge. Bunton and Burrows point out that this discursive shift both de-institutionalises health and opens it up to a much wider range of expertise, so that the contemporary citizen

> is increasingly expected to take note of and act upon the recommendations of a whole range of 'experts' and 'advisers' located in a range of *diffuse* institutional and cultural sites . . . many of which are outside the traditional institutional domains associated with the sick role.
>
> (1995, p. 208)

Perhaps more significantly this developing use of lifestyle involves a considerable extension in our understanding of the notion of consumption – from just goods to all life's activities – and imbues it with previously unsuspected levels of ethical and aesthetic significance (and in both senses undermining the traditional distinction between production and consumption).[9]

A related study is that by Walters of how drug use and persistent criminality might be interrelated (1994). Rather than see drug abuse or criminality as behaviour syndromes in themselves, he suggests that they should be conceptualised as interdependent patterns of dysfunctional retreat which share traits of a common lifestyle. In this perspective lifestyle is not derived from empirical observations alone but is more an analytic construct, or even, as Walters calls it, a caricature: 'A *lifestyle* is defined by three interrelated influences, referred to ... as the "three C's": Conditions, choice and cognition' (1994, p. 6). These provide a set of factors under each heading which act as an interacting network of influences determining whether either form of deviance becomes central to an individual's life concerns.

In this way Walters uses what he calls a lifestyle perspective to see drug abuse as a constitutive feature of what we can call a way of being-in-the-world which is analogous to the idea of audience membership used earlier. Any social policy concerned with change has to address the particular constellation and hierarchy of significance of lifestyle perspectives. Of course, there is a danger here of theorising lifestyles with too much autonomy; lifestyles cannot in themselves generate social consequences but 'Because a lifestyle furnishes an individual with established rules, roles, relationships, and criteria for success and failure, it serves as an alternative to adaptive living' (1994, p. 98).

It is doubtless relevant that this point comes up when noting the approach employed in a book on deviant lifestyles (see also Fiddle 1967). The strongest empirical purchase of a concept of lifestyle, in earlier historical contexts as well as more recently, has always been in relation to minorities who have been forced by ostracism and discrimination to insist upon certain distinctive ways of speaking, dietary and leisure habits as well as values to delineate a mutually sustaining identity (see for example on gay and lesbian lifestyles Whittle (1994), and Wilson (1988) especially Chapter 8). In this respect it becomes virtually impossible to distinguish between lifestyles and subcultures, particularly when fashion in dress and entertainment, etc. becomes a constitutive symbolic vocabulary (as in Hebdige's now classic account of youth subcultures (1979) [10]). It is, however, significant that Jenkins, in his study of working class young men on a Belfast housing estate, used lifestyles rather than subcultures because: 'the concept of subculture ... implies a determinate and often deviant relationship to a notional dominant culture' (1983, p. 41). He argues that a concept of lifestyles does not presuppose values of resistance and more positively emphasises distinctions in practice within a class culture.

I will discuss more fully the significance of lifestyle in relation to cultural theorising in Chapter 10; for now I want to complete this review of some of the ways of using lifestyle in contemporary social analysis by looking at two studies of less self-consciously asserted lifestyle differentiation. The first is a study of how leisure activities, seen as part of a more general lifestyle practice, are used to construct social positions that espouse distinctive values and perspectives (Wynne 1990). The study is directed towards an elaboration of Bourdieu's notions of cultural and economic capital that I will discuss in the next chapter – I will therefore concentrate only on the details of the delineation of lifestyle positions.

In his paper, Wynne proposes that it is possible to distinguish two types of leisure amongst those who live in an expensive suburban estate in northern England, the research consisting of ethnographic interviews and observations as well as quantitative data from a sample survey. Each type is primarily driven by male activities, with women fitting into male patterns, largely it seems because more traditional gendered divisions of labour survive in this largely young and economically successful population. The study report focuses on the use of leisure facilities at a club built on the estate which comprises bars, games rooms, a meeting hall, indoor games facilities and floodlit tennis courts. Wynne argues that ways of using these facilities constitute distinctive leisure practices which are in turn indicators 'that the new middle class use to construct social position' (p. 23).

Within the estate there seems to be a fundamental cleavage between those who left school at 16 and have succeeded through their own entrepreneurial efforts and those whose success was initially based on the credentials of a college education and subsequent professional career. In terms of leisure practices and 'Employing the categories produced by the residents themselves, the first group I have called "the drinkers", and the second "the sporters" ' (p. 25). As the names indicate, the primary focus of difference is in their use of the leisure club where the former group primarily use the bar in male-centred camaraderie, while the latter focus on the social rewards of serious competitive activity. This primary difference is, however, embedded in more general lifestyle values such that the former group favour traditional house decoration, tour company holidays, middle-of-the-road styles of entertainment and steak house restaurants. Sporters place considerably more emphasis on fashionable style, on adventurous challenging entertainment, on personally arranged self-catering holidays and eating at restaurants that fall outside conventional British tastes.

Both groups use the facilities of consumer culture to mark out important aspects of their social identity; they are aware of the differences and each scornful of the other. In summary, the drinkers affirm the traditions of a class culture in order to celebrate their degree of mobility, while their rivals look to more individual achievements in displaying a mastery of cultural skills: 'As such their leisure practices, particularly their involvement with the "learning mode", are essentially attempts at "becoming" ' (p. 34). The struggle between these competing social positions is played out in their respective control of the social spaces of the lounge bar and games courts.

In this study then lifestyle is understood as a very creative use of consumer facilities. Social worlds are organised, structured and imbued with meaning by reference to what sort of people the protagonists are, that is their sense of their own social identity. Put in this way we can appreciate again an earlier theme that lifestyles are reflexive projects: we (and relevant others) can see (however dimly) who we want to be seen to be through how we use the resources of who we are.

In the second study of contemporary lifestyle patterns we turn away from the close focus of ethnographic reporting to a more wide-ranging analysis based upon market research data (Savage *et al*. 1992). Once again the study is set within a theoretical framework derived from Bourdieu's work and as before I will temporarily ignore that dimension to pick out selected details. The authors are concerned with the actual consumption patterns of the middle classes, and use as their source of material an annual survey of the consumption habits of 24,000 adults, supplemented by a more specific study of upper-middle-class and middle-class occupational groups. The most relevant points for our present purposes are given in this slightly lengthy but nevertheless concise summary:

> The TGI survey indicates three salient types of middle-class lifestyle which we have labelled the *ascetic*, the *postmodern*, and the *undistinctive*. All appear to have a distinct social base within the middle classes: the first among the public welfare sector professionals, the second among the private sector professionals and specialist, and the third among managers and government bureaucrats. But these processes interweave with those of gender, age and location.
>
> (Savage *et al*. 1992, p. 127)

The message the authors wish to extract from their data is that a common social position can involve quite different perspectives and values so that effectively lifestyles bespeak quite distinctively different sensibilities. I have carefully chosen to speak of social position in this sentence rather than income because there is a suggestion that the asceticism of what are called intellectuals is to some extent prescribed by poor public sector salaries. This is not, however, a sufficient explanation as with the resources that are available it seems that 'They [ascetics] engage in a number of very active forms of exercise to an extent that is well above the average for ABs as a whole' (p. 109). Otherwise their alcoholic drinking is well below average and their participation in high cultural activities is again above the norm. In contrast, the undistinguished as their name suggests, do not seek out distinctive tastes and while avoiding extremes tend to favour activities that look backwards to more settled and more ordered social worlds.

The third group is called postmodern partly to be provocative about what we shall see as certain celebrations of lifestyle developments, and partly because there does seem an increasing tendency, particularly amongst private sector professionals, to blur conventional stylistic distinctions: 'high extravagance goes along with a culture of the body: appreciation of high cultural forms of art such as opera and classical music exists cheek by jowl with an interest in disco dancing or stock car racing' (p. 108). If the public sector intellectuals of emergent modernity have in the past acted as a vanguard in pioneering the use of cultural resources to mark out a distinctive social position (Brint 1984), it seems that their distinctiveness is now being overtaken. Many elements in the stylistic baggage of those who claimed to be the agents of modernity have been appropriated by later generations and used indiscriminately in ways that subvert (and possibly transcend) the cultural order of modernity.

At this stage we do not have to take a position on how we are to understand this confusing evidence. What is clear from the work I have discussed in the sections of this chapter is that we need something like a concept of lifestyle to describe the social order of the modern world. I have also tried to indicate that this descriptive vocabulary is not just responding to the practical distinctions of everyday life, but is also providing a way of reading those distinctions. And by reading here I suppose I mean thick descriptions [11] of the meanings of things in the play of status, distinction and identity. It is because lifestyles entail theoretical concerns with the interpretation of social and cultural change that in the next chapter I turn to a review of some authors who have influenced our use of a concept of lifestyles.

NOTES

1 Full time gross weekly earnings as at April 1987 for young adults:

	Males	*Females*
Under 18	74	74
18–20	110	96
21–24	152	122

Source: New Earnings Survey (Mintel 1988, p. 9.5)

2 I should acknowledge that the example I have referred to is not perhaps representative of Mintel's more specialist reports on markets such as the green consumer, alcohol and lifestyles, working women, and the market for speciality and ethnic foods (see in particular Mintel 1993).

3 Bocock cites an analogous study by O'Brien and Ford (1988) in which 'age and stage in the marital and reproduction cycle were combined to produce [a] set of life-stages' (Bocock 1993, p. 29), which also function as marketing categories.

4 Perhaps the most complex example of an attempt to map the American population on a status hierarchy that is also stratified by value-outlooks is Mitchell's typology of nine American life-styles (1983). Despite the sophistication of the methodology this study cannot transcend what is by now quite a long tradition in America of psychologizing social trends.

5 I am thinking here of Connerton's suggestion that the body or what he calls bodily practices are one of the main media of memory (1989), an idea I take up again in Chapter 8 on the body as a site for lifestyle.

6 I have referenced Morley's book because it reviews the history and issues well as well as reprinting his own major studies; his reference to my own work in the early chapters is, however, at best superficial and misses what our work has in common.

7 The parallels between audience and market research are intensified when we note that market research uses a hierarchy of adoption stages – from early adopters to laggards – that replicates early work on political persuasion and the diffusion of innovations, see Katz and Lazarsfeld 1955; and Rogers 1983.

8 Radway's study of the meanings women create in their reading of romance literature has rightly been very influential, but the phrase interpretive communities which she uses is in fact a borrowing from Stanley Fish.

9 I am grateful to Roger Burrows and Sarah Nettleton for helping me to grasp the significance of this point.

10 And see also his use of a metaphor of mapping in relation to changing taste in the collection of essays published in 1988.

11 I use this phrase to deliberately signal my own commitment to the interpretive stance recommended amongst others by Clifford Geertz (1973).

Part II

Theorising lifestyles

stems from a situation in which symbolic meaning can be presumed to be widely-known, shared and accepted in a stable community. It is in the world of strangers that characterises modern urban social life that symbolic meaning is infinitely negotiable and continually being re-invented. Lifestyles are then patterned ways of investing certain aspects of everyday life with social or symbolic value; but this also means that they are ways of playing with identity.

It therefore seems to me that what those who have been seen as writing forms of social theory that are relevant to our understanding of lifestyles have in common[1], is a concern with the organisation of secular symbolism. I have used secular here because, although the symbols being used may be treated as sacred by those concerned (thus we might talk of someone worshipping his car) they are not generally seen as representing other-worldly meanings but are tied into this-worldly values. I should also emphasise my focus on the *organisation* of symbolism. I am concerned with how we interpret the structures and processes of material culture, and diffuse as this topic is it does limit the range of possible themes so that, for example, I do not venture into the cognate nature and history of desire (Falk 1994, Chapter 5).

A further reason for seeing the content of lifestyles (that is, what they consist of as well as what they are about) as really being symbolic is that industrialisation has made the world of goods so complex and finely differentiated. Not only has the number of things made vastly increased, but also how they are made available and how they are presented and how they are discussed have all become in themselves further services which are forms of goods and thus purchased in markets. If we add to this summary those goods marketed in a leisure economy which are experiences such as the enjoyment of a landscape or the painted representation of a landscape or a print that reproduces the painted representation, and add to them all the relevant services of marketing and discursive elaboration, then it becomes apparent that to stress the materiality of consumer culture is slightly misleading.

The stuff out of which lifestyles are fashioned is partly something as tangible as the chairs with which you furnish your living room, but is also the shape, the origins of materials and fabrics involved and where and how the production process was staged. There are also further layers of how much you know about all these elements, what sort of messages you think they convey, and where you turn and to whom you listen about how you might change these choices. It is in these ways that lifestyles deal with symbolic competence. Even Lee (1993), who is by no means sympathetic to the 'idealist' implications of stressing the creativity of consumer culture, allows that 'In its passage through the market ... the commodity is itself transformed from an ideal use-value and imagined meaning into the material and symbolic object of lived experience' (Lee 1993, p. 25); and he goes on:

> Although, in its guise as an object of lived culture, the commodity is by no means symbolically fluid, it is certainly symbolically malleable and thus able to assume a variety of meanings and significations according to the contexts of its use and the cultural competences of its users.
>
> (1993, p. 25)

Social theory, when it takes up the significance of lifestyles, is therefore interested in the structures and practices of communities within which competent use of commodities is taken to be a display of membership, the social distribution of different forms of competence and the way they relate to other forms of access to scarce resources, and how the meanings of competent use are intersubjectively negotiated between members. It seems to me that these issues can be divided under three headings and I have therefore written three chapters on different ways of approaching the social organisation of symbolism. It is inevitably an arbitrary framework that is not exhaustive, but I hope it does provide a way of seeing how important streams of theoretical work have fed into the sociological study of lifestyles.

NOTES

1 I have used this form of expression because few of the theorists concerned have explicitly used lifestyles as a topic of concern.

4

Symbolic exchange

I have called this chapter symbolic exchange because I shall be looking at theories in which the use of goods is seen to be embedded in networks of reciprocity. I shall begin by clarifying the use of an idea of competence in the practical business of negotiating lifestyles. I shall do this by turning to possible parallels between the use of a language and the use of symbolic markers in lifestyle practices. In this and succeeding chapters it will become apparent that these parallels have been appealed to in a variety of ways by those concerned with the social theory of modernity.

A notion of communicative competence has been argued to display a mundane ability to communicate with each other through resources that we continually adapt and change in the course of the process of comunication. This model of competent use is in deliberate contrast to more structuralist approaches to language mastery in which a qualitative distinction is drawn between the imperfect performances of everyday life and an inherent competence able to grasp the deep structures of language organisation. While it is not necessary in this context to pursue this debate in detail, it is important to emphasise that I have not been persuaded that the invention of theoretical structures to encompass the variety of human experience is appropriate. Although I do not mean to deny the influence of accounts of the meaning of material goods such as Barthes' study of fashionable clothing (1983), I must make it clear that I refuse to make a principled distinction between the performances of lifestyles and the interpretive ability that informs those choices. Indeed, my stress throughout on the reflexive character of lifestyle practice is meant to indicate that the meaning of different lifestyles is constituted through their unfolding practice.

I believe that my use of a notion of symbolic competence in relation to lifestyle practice is, however, consistent with Douglas and Isherwood's point that 'the very idea of consumption itself has to be set back into the social process. . . . Consumption has to be recognized as an integral part of the same social system that accounts for the drive to work' (1979, p. 4). Their concern is to revise fundamental versions of economic rationality, a project that takes us beyond the confines of this study, but in so doing they make clear that any social theory in this area must begin with the idea that goods as symbols are embedded in broader cultural categories: 'all material possessions carry social meanings and . . . [we must therefore] . . . concentrate a main part of cultural analysis upon their use as communicators' (1979, p. 59). The meanings of goods are grounded in institutional contexts and these provide the context for interpretation.

For Douglas and Isherwood the uses of goods express social knowledge because, in the same way that individuality presupposes the cultural resources through which it is expressed, so personal consumption (a lifestyle) of goods is 'the visible part of culture. They are arranged in vistas and hierarchies that can give play to the full range of discrimination of which the human mind is capable' (1979, p. 66). In a later collection (1987) Mary Douglas has brought together a number of studies focusing on alcoholic drinking as it is embedded in the social organisation of local realities. Deliberately turning away from a more conventional pathological focus in which drinking is seen as aberrant or destructive, here alcohol is seen as an integral element in the organisation of social occasions, rituals of social identity and systems of social control. In these studies the use of alcohol is not described through lifestyle concepts so much as themes in local cultures, perhaps allowing more easily the introduction of an idea of how material goods can symbolise utopian alternatives.

Amongst the scarce resources that are necessarily used in all cultures to mark out differences in power and status are what Douglas calls periodicities – the extent and immediacy of routine concern with life-sustaining activities (Douglas 1970). Essential to the privileges of high social status is the ability to command others to, or command technological resources which, enable the individual to escape the constraints of periodicity. Part of what I was trying to express in the introduction about the symbolic character of mass society is the idea that periodicities are becoming increasingly arbitrary and artificial. Rising standards of living mean that markets and technologies are more broadly accessible but

> Seeking a relationship between perodicities and status is an exercise in structural analysis . . . On the analogy of a tune unfolding its pattern in a temporal scheme, the goods reveal their usefulness in the total scheme of periodicities in which they serve.
>
> (Douglas and Isherwood 1979, p. 123)

We have then in this perspective a way of seeing lifestyles as ways of mediating technologies, structures of relationships and symbolic meanings. We cannot glibly read off a set of names for lifestyles as marketing research would like to be able to do, but we are beginning to see how the symbols used in lifestyle practice are in networks of symbolic exchange. Douglas's sociological approach to economic behaviour makes clear that the activities I have described as consumption are *modes of cultural production*. Through the manipulation of and discrimination between goods we are forming distinctive types of social relationships with their own logics of reciprocity and aesthetics of appreciation. It is these latter institutional dynamics that are the hallmarks of the type of sociological theorising we associate with Georg Simmel.

Simmel too, in his major book on the philosophy of money (1978, see in particular Chapter 6 for ideas I go on to discuss), is concerned to transcend the discourse of economics. In the preface he affirms that 'not a single line of these investigations is meant to be a statement about economics' (quoted in Frisby 1992, p. 80). He is concerned rather to treat exchange as a social fact, something that has to be understood as a network of social relationships (although it also exists in other discourses). The fact that these relationships can be predicated upon the use of money introduces further levels of symbolic, and thereby social, complexity: 'Money is "possible" . . . only once men embrace a "relativistic world view" in which objects have value exclusively in terms of their exchange value in relation to other objects' (Shad 1990, p. 299).

Money therefore transforms objects from their intrinsic meaning to acting as elements in a new, cultural discourse that is independent of functions and individual tastes. Simmel illustrates the social character of changing economic relationships by pointing to two further consequences (in the process illustrating the two sidedness of any relationship). The first is that in the modern world as money, in all its various forms, becomes more important – so that the social interdependence of economic union becomes stronger – we as individual participants can remain more distanced when compared to the economic relationships of traditional society. And similarly, although the complex differentiation of production renders consumers more dependent on market supply, even so any one consumer is more free to pick and choose amongst his/her suppliers (see also Simmel 1991a).

I have begun this review of aspects of Simmel's thought by making some points about his theory of the nature of money for three reasons. First, because it leads into a fuller discussion of the social organisation of using goods and particularly the institution of fashion. Second, the particular character of how Simmel theorises money also introduces the most frequently commented upon character of his work – that nothing exists and has a meaning purely by itself. All social phenomena are *forms* of relationship but also and simultaneously exist as the *content* of other forms of association. It is this realisation of the impossibility of fixing a basic level of reality that determines Simmel's definition of the project of sociology – the study of sociation. A third reason for beginning with the theory of money is that it also introduces the theme of modernity which is the essential backdrop to all other aspects of Simmel's concerns.

I will expand on each of these points as they may help to bear on a theoretical grasp of the significance of lifestyles, beginning with the social institution of fashion. Fashion is an appropriate topic for our concerns because it is clearly a mode of action that has been stimulated by the development of consumer industries. The dynamics of change in different modes of fashion surely mirrors broader processes of lifestyle formation. I will return to these issues but for now note that for Simmel fashion is not exclusive to modernity, but is a perennial illustration of his theme of the interdependence of form and content (1971a). Being in fashion both provides a badge of inclusion and incorporation confirming your social identity as at the same time allowing individuals to differentiate themselves from others. Nedelmann (1990) has suggested that in the interaction between these poles of imitation and differentiation Simmel is using a metaphor of a circle rather than the more conventional image of cause and effect, and 'this would imply that these processes create their own momentum: they are, to use a term which is hard to translate, *eigendynamisch*' (p. 244).

The ebb and flow of consolidation and distinction that characterises the process of fashion does not, however, operate on only one level. In a socially stratified society it is made more complex by elites seeking to abandon fashions as soon as they are imitated by lower-class groups, so that there is a vertical process of exchange between classes as well as horizontal processes within a class. In particular, students of fashion have to be concerned with the social structure of audiences, with the different interests and concerns of those who are innovators as opposed to middle-of-the-roaders and those who are laggards. A particularly interesting social type thrown up by worlds of fashion, already noted, is the dandy or aesthete who prides (initially) himself on his grasp of the nuances of fashionable discrimination. It is because this role of innovation is on the edges of established conventions that Simmel makes a connection to a form of life '[that] the demi-monde is so frequently a pioneer in matters of fashion is due to its peculiarly uprooted form of life' (1971a, p. 311).

Fashion is then a mode of social action that is both circular and transitional. At any point in the circle you are always in the process of transition to another; in the same way that, as he clarifies in another paper (Simmel 1994), crossing a bridge or going through a door is always both an event now and a process of transition. The dynamics of this process are not fixed or immutable but are greatly stimulated by the defining innovation of modernity – the metropolitan city. Here the dynamics of fashionable change are vastly accelerated, and there are opportunities for industries to supply objects of fashionable discrimination to mass markets: 'The more an article becomes subject to rapid changes of fashion, the greater the demand for *cheap* products of its kind' (1971a, p. 318). The social institution of fashion serves then two roles for Simmel, the first as a vehicle for themes in his social theory and the second as integral element in his account of metropolitan life. It is to this dimension that I now turn.

While Simmel in his best-known essay, that on metropolitan life (1971b), is often read as providing another version of the loss of community thesis commonly associated with Tönnies, I think his account of modernity is considerably more complex than that would suggest (see Frisby 1985). It is clear, however, that the metropolis is seen as the engine of modernity. And in particular the metropolis is seen as the focus of new forms of civilised life; it is therefore a world of taste and discrimination in which consumption is overwhelmingly more important than production. The metropolis is, however, as with everything in Simmel, janus-faced – the individual is never more lonely or isolated than when in a crowd and the emptiness of nature only becomes aesthetic when seen through the prism of urban complexity (on the duality of boundaries in Simmel and particularly in relation to metropolitan life see Weinstein and Weinstein 1993).

The metropolis is therefore a sociological entity that appropriates space rather than a spatial entity that underlies social relations. Sociologically, the metropolis is mediated through symbolism – it is a life-world in which symbols mutually refer in ever more complex layers of association and in which the play of meanings can only be understood reflexively and as a constant process of innovation. The increasingly differentiated world of goods of modernity is not a simple process of enrichment, but neither is it straightforward alienation. The cultural terrain of the metropolis simultaneously offers new potentials for individuals to enhance their subjectivity.

Grasping this constant shifting of focus is necessary to appreciate the essay on style which touches most closely on lifestyle practices (1991b; see also Nedelmann 1991). Here Simmel draws an important distinction between applied and pure art, the former is practical and is: 'a means – which therefore has an end outside itself – while the work of art is never a means, but a work closed in on itself' (1991b, p. 67). Practical works are not inferior to the disinterested autonomy of art works, but it mistakes their function to treat them as though they are art. Rather, functional objects should be appreciated for the common language they necessarily share. Precisely because they are stylised, that is they draw upon continuities in form, they can provide a degree of integration in which excessive subjectivity is calmed: 'What drives modern man so strongly to style is the unburdening and concealment of the personal, which is the essence of style' (1991b, p. 69).

Simmel's account of the meaning of symbolic goods seeks to locate meanings in the reciprocity of structural forms, but not to treat reciprocity as an exchange of counters. In his view, in the organisation and use of symbolic goods we are not dealing with them as representations but as networks of relationship. In particular, the dialectic of objectification of material culture and the subjectification of personal meaning is driven by the engine of the division of labour. This should be understood as the specialization of symbolic exchange as described above, rather than just differentiated processes of production (see Simmel 1978, pp. 453–79). The multiplicity of lifestyles in the mass economies of the twentieth century can perhaps be captured by the analogy of the sorceror's apprentice. Simmel says that while we live within a single style of life, or a single language, local social order appears inevitable. It is only with a plurality of options that we are forced into a reflexive stance towards all our options. The accelerated pace of change in a mass economy breeds its own necessity for further and more complex differentiation.

A process of accelerated change is complemented by both a fragmentation of social forms and a feeling of the necessary instability of symbolic orders. As Frisby has pointed out: 'Fashion is, then, part of the more general process of accentuation of time-consciousness in a distinctive sense' (1985, p. 99). It is because the inhabitants of mass society are forced into an awareness of how quickly things change, and therefore how quickly future possibilities will be manifested, that there is a concentration of social consciousness upon the transitory: 'we only denote as fashion that which disappears as quickly as it emerged' (1985, p. 99). An unlikely echo of some elements in these thoughts, which also begins from an emphasis upon the emancipation of value from any grounding in the reality of use or function, can be found in the work of Baudrillard. In the opening sentence of the most recent book of his to be translated into English, he declares that 'Symbolic exchange is no longer the organising principle of modern society' (Baudrillard 1993, p. 1). The reason is that the transitoriness of symbolic meaning Simmel predicted has become culturally dominant: 'Everywhere, in every domain, a single form predominates: reversibility, cyclical reversal and annulment put an end to the linearity of time, language, economic exchange, accumulation and power' (p. 2).

Baudrillard, too, points to the social institution of fashion in contemporary modernity as a spectacular display of more general processes of accelerated change and the alienation of meaning: 'The acceleration of the simple play of signifiers in fashion becomes striking, to the point of enchanting us – the enchantment and vertigo of the loss of every system of reference' (1993, p. 87). There are in this quotation two claims. First, that the social determinations of meaning have been overtaken so that the signs and symbols of fashionable display circulate without any logic. As he goes on to say: 'There is no longer any determinacy internal to the signs of fashion, hence they become free to commute and permutate without limit' (p. 87). Second, that the consequent meaninglessness is not horrifying chaos as we might expect, but is, instead, 'enchanting' – a form of hallucination I discuss again in Chapter 6.

The essence of Baudrillard's argument is that the signifiers of economic value – that is units of currency – have been divorced from any necessary relationship with the signifieds of real value. This has been caused by twin processes of the development of a consumption economy, particularly in the later twentieth century, and speculation in money as a good in its own right, so that 'Freed from the market itself, it [money] becomes an autonomous simulacrum, relieved of every message and every signification of exchange, becoming a message in itself and exchanging amongst itself' (1993, p. 22; see also Shad 1990 linking Simmel and Baudrillard). The rootlessness of money is the most visible instance of a more general revolution in the ways in which it has been presumed that the social materiality of objects informs or determines their meaning. In consequence, we cannot refer outside the systems of communication: 'The reality principle corresponded to a certain stage of the law of value. Today the whole system is swamped with indeterminacy, and every reality is absorbed by the hyperreality of the code and simulation' (Baudrillard 1993, p. 2).

At its most apocalyptic this means that 'political, social, historical, economic, etc., reality has already incorporated the hyperrealist dimension of simulation so that we are now living entirely within the "aesthetic" hallucination of reality' (1993, p. 74; see also on the hyperreality of contemporary society Eco 1987 and Baudrillard 1988). The necessary consequence, of society moving beyond the capitalist economy that Marx analysed through the labour theory of value, is that we move into a world of dreams (or nightmares) driven by the sensuality of representation. The relationship of signifier and signified, or more precisely the order of representation, is obviously crucial to Baudrillard's account of contemporary cultural history and I shall therefore briefly describe what he calls the three orders of simulacra (cf. 1993, Chapter 2; see also 1983).

To simulate is to represent, to provide something that stands for, and simulacra or means of representation only come into being for Baudrillard with the loss of stability of traditional or feudal social orders. The first order of simulacra therefore exists from the Renaissance to the Industrial Revolution and is called the counterfeit because signs pretend to imitate nature. This order is replaced by the mechanisation of production in industrialisation which meant that signs were generated for their market value. But the logic of this process is that objects lose their intrinsic meaning and lead to a third order. In this order, simulacra, and here picking up on Benjamin's paper on the meaning of the work of art in an era of mass production (1970), become designed for reproducibility: 'Production itself has no meaning: its social finality is lost in the series. Simulacra prevail over history' (Baudrillard 1993, p. 56).

So, we can now see more clearly how the social institution of fashion exemplifies some of these theses. Fashionable items, be they clothes, furniture or holiday destinations, do not derive their prestige from the job they do but from the way that they do it. Fashion is therefore a level of representation that does not refer outside its own discourses. Although Baudrillard distinguishes between what he calls the 'light' signs of the spheres of fashion already mentioned, and the 'heavy' signs of more traditional institutions of politics, economics and science, etc. 'it remains the case that every sphere tends, unequally but simultaneously, to merge with models of simulation, of differential and indifferent play, the structural play of value' (1993, p. 87; and in the process of the argument fatally undermining the possibility of any form of critical discourse). It is the irrationality of fashion that makes it enchanting, precisely because fashionable discriminations are not grounded in material reality, they are emphatically spectacular signs. In using and responding to others' use we are enjoying the drama of presentation and change for its own sake, and it is this self-sufficiency that gives an aesthetic hallucination of reality: 'fashion aims for a theatrical sociality, and delights in itself' (Baudrillard 1993, p. 94).

Were he to stop there Baudrillard's analysis would seem to confirm all the worst fears of those who see lifestyles, which are after all the social organisation and exemplification of fashionable discriminations, as ephemeral mystifications (a view that Baudrillard himself often seems to support). While purporting to give meaning and purpose to life, fashion would be, in Shakespeare's phrase, merely a confusion of sound and fury signifying nothing.

Baudrillard does, however, see a subversive potential even in excessive sociality: 'Beyond the rational and the irrational, beyond the beautiful and the ugly, the useful and the useless, it is this immorality in relation to all criteria, the frivolity which at times gives fashion its subversive force' (1993, p. 94). There is, then, in the structural play of self-referential signification an anarchy of signs that is threatening through its very lack of order: 'Fashion is immoral . . . [and this] . . . is power's hell, the hell of the relativity of all signs which all power is forced to crush in order to maintain its own signs' (1993, p. 98). This idea of the potency of subversive meaninglessness is why certain aspects of Baudrillard's thought have been taken up in avant garde provocations, and why certain aspects of the lifestyles of the marginal have begun to be seen as a new post-socialist revolutionary politics.

The theorists discussed in this section have in their very different ways clearly moved any account of lifestyles away from the specificities, for example, of the proportion of the population owning compact disc players and joining and regularly attending a health club. Instead, the importance and meaning of these activities is argued to only be comprehensible in the context of a more wide-ranging account of the dynamics of value in modernity. The fact that people attach importance to their own and others' lifestyles must be seen as part of the way in which viable social order is being negotiated when many of the grounding structures of tradition have been knocked away. The question of how successful lifestyles are as stabilising mechanisms we will have to leave for further discussion; it is clear that there are strong strains of pessimism (although not unmitigated) in the theoretical accounts I have described so far. In the next chapter I will consider alternative views on the accumulation rather than the negotiation of symbolic value.

5

Symbolic capital

In the previous chapter I discussed social theories which have concentrated on the networks of exchange that are organised around treating consumption goods as symbols in modern society. I noted at several points how the metaphor of economic value was being used to illuminate symbolic value. This metaphor carries us on to the types of theory to be described in this chapter. The reason is that repositories of value, whether they are objects such as paintings or symbols of money or access to potential such as the rights to a future crop, can, as well as being exchanged, be accumulated. They become capital which, as the Marxist tradition has so forcefully emphasised, is inextricably linked to all forms of institutionalised power. It seems then that the social organisation of consumption, which we loosely refer to as lifestyles, will be intimately bound up with the persistence of social structure, as I recognised at the beginning of the first chapter, and we therefore need to consider more carefully the dynamics of this process.

The logic of a transition from exchange to capital has not escaped the writers already mentioned. Douglas and Isherwood point out that although differences in consumption styles associated with vast differences in income in traditional societies are predictably massive, patterns are not so clear-cut in developed economies. It is not clear that a particular style of taste will be associated with high or lower class position. Instead Douglas and Isherwood suggest stratifying a modern society by the dominant type of goods consumed. First a set of staples, then a technology set based on goods produced through industrial production, and finally a set of goods characterised as information produced by the service sector. They argue that those who consume a disproportionately large amount of the third set constitute a class who will restrict entry by controlling access to the resources with which to manipulate information goods.

Members of this group do so because the status they derive from mastery of information brings disproportionately large rewards; and because they will be able to use that mastery to manipulate symbolic values further privileging their own tastes and discriminations: 'The contention is that entry into the services sector of the productive system is made easier by prior entry into the social class that consumes the information set of goods' (Doulgas and Isherwood 1979, pp. 182–3). This is the advantage enjoyed by

> the individual who wants to be highly paid, who can see that earnings are high in the services sector, and whose private consumption habits have trained him in an immensely fine judgement of names in some part of the range of valued information goods and services.
>
> (1979, p. 183)

It is then not just that the accumulation of goods provides a form of capital which can be manipulated to secure advantages through generations; but that *the knowledge of how to discriminate* within a world of goods is a further form of capital, this time symbolic, that generates equivalent or even more substantial rewards. More generally we can argue that in the course of modernity a new class of professionals or intellectuals has emerged and become powerful; and that this group has strong reasons for attaching importance to, as well as being good at, manipulating criteria of discrimination – that is, lifestyles.

Although a number of authors have pursued this theme it has tended to be commonly associated with the work of Pierre Bourdieu, and particularly with one of his major studies, that of cultural discriminations (1984). There are other more general connections between the work of Douglas and Bourdieu, although neither consistently references the other. Both are interested, for example, in the significance of language competence as a model for all modes of symbolisation;[1] and both claim to be seeking for a middle way between the abstract logic of structural determinations and the atomising subjectivity of personal creativity. Both of these points inform Bourdieu's theory of social action and need to be clarified before I can more directly consider his account of consumption choices (as a particular mode of action) in contemporary France.

In understanding others' actions Bourdieu takes it for granted that we cannot take their explanations as sufficient. The reason is given by a commitment to what he calls objectivist theory which asks what are the conditions that make subjects' experience possible. This traditional sociological move is not, however, sufficient. An objectivist cannot presume that the world they inhabit is the same for all its inhabitants. He argues that an adequate theory of practice will also have to ask about the conditions of representation which underlie any objectivist account (this summary is largely based on Bourdieu 1977). There is therefore the danger of an infinite regress which can be resolved only by self-consciousness about the relationship between theory and the actions it attempts to explain. A self-consciousness that is expressed through a recognition of the necessity of a dialectic between the structural conditions of possibility and actors' use of those possibilities.

I think this captures what Bourdieu means by the reflexive character of social practice. I shall shortly argue that this use of the reflexive has major limitations and attempt to show in the next part of the chapter the implications of a different use of the reflexive for our understanding of lifestyles. For now, it is important to see that for Bourdieu there is a refusal to see social life as just the consequence of actors following a set of rules, because 'To substitute *strategy* for the *rule* is to reintroduce time, with its rhythm, its orientation, its irreversibility' (1977, p. 9; emphasis in original). At the same time there is a complementary refusal to see actors as creatively autonomous. In seeking to resolve this contradiction Bourdieu turns to the analogy of language. He begins with a distinction between language, *langue*, and speech, *parole*, associated with Saussure. Bourdieu is, as one should expect, dismissive of what he sees as Saussure's objectivism in relegating speech, and social practice more generally, to be merely execution of the rules of language. Indeed, he sees the failing here to be a more general inadequacy of social theory: 'It would not be difficult to show that the construction of the concept of culture . . . or social structure . . . similarly implies the construction of a notion of conduct as execution' (1977, p. 24).

He insists, however, that the alternative is not to fall into the trap of extreme subjectivism, which he associates with American ethnomethodologists. It is instead to move towards a dialectical relationship 'between the objective relations of the language and the dispositions making up linguistic competence' (1977, p. 84), and this is a '*dialectic of the internalization of externality and the externalization of internality*' (p. 72; emphasis in original). This dialectic is not peculiar to the practice of language but is equally true of the conceptual opposition between the social structure and the individual – and thus in this dialectic he is, in his view, transcending traditional modes of structuralism (more generally on language in structures of social power see Bourdieu 1991).

The way in which this dialectic is, if you like, institutionalised for Bourdieu is through his centrally important concept of the habitus. The idea of the habitus is that they are 'systems of durable, transposable *dispositions*, structured structures predisposed to function as structuring structures' (1977, p. 72; emphasis in original); that is a mechanism through which the objective requirements of cultural order are inscribed as predictable courses of action for individuals. 'The habitus is the source of these series of moves which are objectively organized as strategies without being the product of a genuine strategic intention' (1977, p. 73).

For Bourdieu, an important illustration of this process is provided by structures of gendered relationships in general, and their exemplification, in particular, in the organisation of space in a traditional Berber household in Algeria (study reprinted in Douglas 1973). In charting a series of oppositions between male and female spaces both within the house and between interior and exterior Bourdieu may seem to be following structuralist principles, but in his own view he was rather seeing how the forms of the lived world become unproblematically comprehensible for its inhabitants: 'the habitus represents a conceptual framework describing a "perception-enabling prism" which houses the various social dispositions that, according to its particular logic, allow for the cultural classification of the social world' (Lee 1993, p. 31).

Once again the example of language use provides a conceptual model to which we can refer in trying to grasp how the habitus operates, an example that leads to a particular vocabulary of exposition. Thus Jenkins, when seeking to describe the principles of the habitus, slips easily into ideas drawn from the philosophy of language: 'Socially competent performances are produced as a matter of routine, without explicit reference to a body of codified knowledge, and without the actors necessarily "knowing what they are doing" ' (Jenkins 1992, p. 76). While this of course leaves the nature and extent of the creativity of individual 'dispositions' unclear, more positively it does put the contingencies of local circumstance in an historical context: 'The habitus as a shared body of dispositions, classificatory categories and generative schemes is, if it nothing else, the outcome of collective history ... experienced as the taken-for-granted, axiomatic necessity of objective reality' (Jenkins 1992, p. 80).

The habitus provides for Bourdieu the crucial link between the objectivity of social reality and the subjectivity of personal experience. We should, therefore, be able to use a notion of habitus to explain what at first appears to be the idiosyncratic variety of cultural choices:

> In fact ... the different ways of relating to realities and fictions ... are very closely linked to the different possible positions in social space and, consequently, bound up with the systems of dispositions (habitus) characteristic of the different classes and class fractions.
>
> (Bourdieu 1984, pp. 5–6)

The important point is that the phrase 'bound up with' suggests that these characteristic tastes are more than the descriptive reports of market research. Rather, tastes are the consequence of generative principles which define for the actors concerned meaningful universes. We are then led on to the crucial argument that 'Lifestyles are thus the systematic products of habitus, which, perceived in their mutual relations through the schemes of the habitus, become sign systems that are socially qualified (as "distinguished", "vulgar", etc.)' (Bourdieu 1984, p. 172; see also Jenks 1993).

I have emphasised at several points that the habitus generates what Bourdieu calls 'that naturalization of its own arbitrariness ... [through] the dialectic of the objective chances and the agents' aspirations out of which arises the *sense of limits*, commonly called the *sense of reality*' (1977, p. 164; emphasis in original). But it is precisely because the cognitive order of a particular habitus is arbitrary, that, in its operation, it will lead to systematic distortion, what he calls misrecognition, of the world at hand. Inevitably and importantly it follows that: 'As all members assume and become aware of reality through and within culture, they inevitably and unknowingly have the structure of existing power relations thrust upon them' (Jenks 1993, p. 13). The burden of the use of thrust here is that the misrecognition entailed in the sway of an habitus is a form of what Bourdieu calls symbolic violence.

One might think that such is the necessity for the cognitive order of a habitus that it suffers from the problem of Althusser's ideological state apparatus – that is, that it is so suffocatingly powerful that any form of cultural variety let alone opposition becomes an inexplicable anomaly. Bourdieu does, however, allow for the possibility of struggles between and within social classes over boundary distinctions around what can be questioned, and what is so taken-for-granted that it is beyond discussion. While it is unclear to me how this struggle is sustained it is undoubtedly related to what most of us would expect to see as the practice of symbolic violence – that is the ways in which class differences in access to the acquisition of skills are reproduced through generations.

In practice this means that symbolic mastery is privileged by those who are culturally dominant and restricted to favoured groups, while those excluded are forced to concentrate upon what he calls practical mastery. Thus he has attempted to show that 'the dominant pedagogic work, particularly in secondary education, will lean heavily on the *implicit* inculcation of that symbolic mastery' (Jenkins 1992, p. 108; emphasis in original; see also Bourdieu and Passeron 1990). Given the nature of the different types of skills being made available, his subsequent argument follows: that aesthetic discriminations and attitudes necessary for the cultural discourse of the privileged are part of the habitus of those with symbolic mastery (see 1984, in particular Chapter 1), and thus that the disadvantaged are violently forced into the reproduction of that which disadvantages (see also Rigby 1991, Chapter 4; Fowler 1994).

It should be clear, then, that the violence employed in symbolic reproduction is directed towards the defence of the privileges of those who are powerful enough to so use it, and that therefore those privileges are a form of goods that constitute a mode of capital: 'Without entering into detailed analysis, it must suffice to point out that academic qualifications are to cultural capital what money is to economic capital' (Bourdieu 1977, p. 187). Jenkins has pointed out that this both makes culture of central importance to the social order of the modern world, and puts it in the curious position of being both the goal and the means of class struggle: 'Culture, and the institutions of cultural production, categorisation and registration (legitimation), are things *with* which people fight, *about* which they fight, and the ground *over* which they fight' (1992, p. 120; emphasis in original).[2]

The main reason for this epochal importance is that the inter-personal strategies of traditional social order have been objectified in modernity into new forms of social capital. And thus, going back to the starting point of my discussion of Bourdieu, these forms of capital are themselves the subject of discursive (cultural) competence: 'The intellectuals (the dominated fraction of the dominant class), therefore, use the logic of symbolic systems to produce distinctions which contribute to the reproduction of the existing relations between classes and class fractions' (Featherstone 1991, p. 89). I have tried to show how the theme of cultural capital is the ways in which distinctive cultural competence is objectified in qualifications, in possessions and activities as well as the relevant critical discourses with which to appropriate these symbolic goods (see DiMaggio (1994) for a review of studies using notions of cultural capital to explain social stratification).

I hope it will have become clear why I have chosen to discuss Bourdieu's study of contemporary French lifestyles, and the theor-etical rationale for the study, under the heading of symbolic capi-tal. Bourdieu is concerned with the social organisation of the acquisition and manipulation of cultural (or symbolic goods) because this organisation is held to be structured in ways that are homologous with the social structures of economic capital. Although we have to bear in mind the important qualification that the upper class is never homogeneous, there being a crucial distinction between those who acquire their cultural capital through inheritance and those who acquire it purely through edu-cational qualifications.

The actual practices of consumption, that is acquisition and manipulation, are to be treated as the display of the mastery of a code of communication, also to be known as an 'aesthetic dispo-sition, the most rigorously demanded of all the terms of entry which the world of legitimate culture (always tacitly) imposes' (Bourdieu 1984, p. 28). Knowing what these practices will mean to, and mean to you when done by, significant others functions much as the communicative competence displayed in language use: 'one can see how it is that the manner of using symbolic goods, especially those regarded as the attributes of excellence, constitutes one of the key markers of "class" and also the ideal weapon in strategies of distinction' (1984, p. 66).

What follows from this theoretical framework, particularly in terms of how we are to interpret the world of stylistic distinction that we all know so well? I shall give a number of answers largely drawn from the book called *Distinction*. The first point is that it is possible to predict that the different elements of class-based lifestyles will be coherent; that is, that knowing someone's taste in a particular area, such as the type of painting or music they enjoy, will allow analysts to predict with reasonable confidence what their choices would be in another area such as food or attitudes to birth control. This sort of suggestion is often felt to be scandalous because it offends individuals' beliefs that their choices are uniquely bound in with their personality. Of course the more one knows then the finer stylistic discriminations that are both possible and necessary, but if one stays at a fairly general level of analysis then the sort of mapping Bourdieu provides of three class levels of taste – upper, lower and intermediate – seems to work. The idea that these are enclosed cultural universes certainly seems to explain why friendships and marriages rarely stray across lifestyle boundaries.

The second point, contained I suppose in what I have just said, is that the metaphor of mapping suggests that the analytic focus can be progressively refined to give an increasingly detailed 'picture'. See for example the diagram of 'the food space' (1984, p. 186) in which cross-cutting variables such as the presence or absence of cultural and economic capital, gender, amount of spare time for food preparation and social status are correlated. These factors are held to generate patterns of taste between those who like rich, strong, fatty, salty foods as compared to those who prefer refined, light, healthy, natural-sweet foods. Again, the logic of the analysis is that the same increasingly detailed account of patterns of taste can be generated in any area of lifestyle discrimination. In doing so we are, however, instructed by the third point to remember that objects acquire meaning, as do words, through their associations with other objects not in themselves, and thus 'detective stories, science fiction or strip cartoons may be entirely prestigious cultural assets or be reduced to their ordinary value, depending on whether they are associated with avant-garde literature or music . . . or combine to form a constellation typical of middle-brow taste' (p. 88).

In recognising the play of these nuances Bourdieu is reminding us of the significance he attaches to strategies of social interaction rather than robotic rule-following. It also allows him to develop the further idea that those with cultural capital are both able and confident enough to experiment with established taste boundaries, while it is the petit-bourgeois intermediaries who, lacking either the insulation of ignorance or the self-confidence bred by discourses of education, tend to be most deferential to the orthodoxies of conventional taste.[3] There is, however, a more substantial methodological significance in all this. The book on habitus and lifestyles is based upon Bourdieu's analysis of previously gathered survey materials. He believes that it is possible to use his analytic armoury of distinctions between economic and cultural capital etc., to chart the determinations of systematic choice. At the same time the construction of 'social space as an objective space' – necessary to 'escape from the subjectivist illusion' – 'is a provisional objectivism which ... reifies what it describes' (1984, p. 246).

The fourth point is therefore that analysis of lifestyles has to transcend their objective forms and remain eternally sensitive to the interplay of struggle between competing classes and class fractions. Particularly relevant to the articulation of these struggles is the development of discourse specialists which we can also call cultural intermediaries (and none more so than Bourdieu and his followers who are able to position themselves as the ultimate deconstructionists of discourse in 'reading' others' delusions of taste). These are figures who, socially uprooted by the mobility's of the proliferating division of labour of late capitalism, are particularly receptive to the advice of those who comment upon changes in fashion in music, food, furnishings, etc. The experts are published in a growing periodical literature and other forms of media commentary devoted to lifestyle advice; although advice is often given from a stance of deploring excessive lifestyle concern.

The rise of new modes of expertise is then the fifth point to take from Bourdieu's work and is a theme that has been emphasised by Mike Featherstone (1991, Chapters 3 and 4; see also the discussion of Bauman in the next chapter). Their role stems from the space for their expertise opened up by new industries of cultural production and the deracination of cultural signifiers stressed in the previous part of the chapter. As Lee has emphasised:

'While it is certainly true that commodities ... are used by people as symbolic co-ordinates for the mapping and construction of social relations, this should not lead us to assume that the powers of advertisers, designers, marketers, or point-of-sale strategists in general are negligible in the discursive framing of these co-ordinates.

(1993, pp. 38–9)

Bourdieu's theoretical approach to the meaning of lifestyle choices is clearly important because it helps us to understand why socio-structural distinctions have in the later stages of modernity been increasingly articulated through cultural forms. More particularly, any account of power and the exploitation of structured privilege in post-industrial societies will have to use his notions of symbolic violence and symbolic capital (see for example the studies collected in Lamont and Fournier 1992). Using this framework he is able to suggest why different modes of capital acquisition (both economic and cultural capital) within a class will generate different constellations of taste, with quite distinctively different expectations towards sport, diet, the arts, furnishings and leisure activities in general. Bourdieu's work is also an essential contribution to any account of both the reflexive consciousness and ideological blind-spots of intellectual fractions in societies of spectacle.

All this reads very interestingly and has been extensively quoted and cited by others writing on aspects of contemporary social structure and change. One cannot, however, avoid the suspicion that the relationship between the fascinating empirical detail and the theoretical edifice on which this detail is 'hung' is at best arbitrary. In much the way that marketing research identifies details of social patterns of taste and then hangs descriptive labels on these patterns as 'explanations', so Bourdieu's reading of survey data identifies patterns that can inevitably be illuminated by an agile mind. Whether or not these explanations are convincing depends upon what else is known by the reader of what they take to be relevant structural factors.

This it seems to me lies behind the criticisms made by Savage and his associates in their study of middle-class lifestyles (1992) briefly discussed in the third chapter. While they agree that 'Bourdieu's main contribution is to show that the dominant and subordinate groups within the middle classes are engaging in endless though reasonably genteel battles to assert their own identities, social positions and worth' (p. 100), they do not accept that

Bourdieu's specification of these battles corresponds to empirical reality outside France. The reasons for this view are that 'there is no *conceptual* (or empirical) space in Bourdieu's framework for the "organisation man" ' (p. 102). These are people who are dedicated in ways the authors identify in their own reading of survey data to 'inconspicuous consumption'. A second reason for Bourdieu's empirical arbitrariness is in their view a confusing lack of precision in his use of a concept of economic capital and 'A final weakness in Bourdieu's account is his neglect of household and gender relations, which, . . . may be becoming a more central determinant of middle-class formation' (p. 103).

More significantly, I feel that Bourdieu's use of reflexivity is impoverished. I noted earlier that his use of the reflexive stems from the dialectical character of social action, and we have subsequently seen how this is exemplified in relation to his account of lifestyle formation. He is, however, necessarily committed to the view that the habitus from which they spring defines the meaning and validity of lifestyle choices – he is in effect unable to escape the structuralism he claims to have transcended. The very prescriptive determinism of his concept of habitus does not allow him to fully appreciate the ways in which actors may and will play with these choices as ironic commentaries on their own styles of life. I would suggest that a full sense of reflexivity must address the ways in which a use of discursive representation constitutes, and thereby necessarily develops, that which it is bringing into being (the several uses of reflexivity have been clearly set out in Czyzewski 1994; on the significance of the term for theories of social action see Sandywell 1996).

For Bourdieu, despite his talk of strategies in social action, the commitment to deny subjectivist illusions means that the objective reality of a habitus necessarily determines individual actions. To revise the relevant habitus to a more precise specification of a class fraction is only to embark upon a potentially infinite regress. The major reason for Bourdieu's difficulties in this respect is of course his prior theoretical commitment to the need to retain a belief in the objective reality of social structural alignments independent of actors' use of those alignments. His difficulties are, however, made more vivid in relation to lifestyles because it is as if he underestimates his own emphasis upon the objectifications of capital: 'For many people, Bourdieu's view of the role of culture in modern society is not only very pessimistic but also rather outdated' (Rigby 1991, p. 123). To assume that objectifications are only displays of a lesser or greater mastery of cultural codes is to presume that there is a pre-existing and unchanging hierarchy of codes – or perhaps more accurately, it is to presume that culture is an inescapable environment which envelops social action in the way that social structures envelop individual experience.

The logic of his own analysis of the reflexive strategies of social action is that any notion of culture – as a stable framework for social action – is necessarily fragmented. A central element in why there has been an increasing interest in lifestyle practices in later modernity is that an established hierarchy of cultural codes is perhaps a too limited view of cultural history but is certainly being overturned by contemporary practice. The details of the objectifications of socio-structural distinctions are still to be charted in particular instances, but what is clear is that (as Donald has said of the need to re-write Bourdieu's theories of the forma-tion of subjectivity) 'The process involves a much more complex dynamic between the pedagogic and the performative' (Donald 1993, p. 52).

I have emphasised that for Bourdieu the significance of cul-tural discrimination is based on the rise of a new class of expertise, and that Bourdieu's model of the relationship between class and lifestyle allows for the possibility of changing class formations and distinctive differences between class fractions. This aspect of his work has proved attractive to Lash and Urry in their studies of changes in the political economy of capitalism in later mod-ernity (1987 and 1994). In their first book in which they hypoth-esise the emergence of a new phase of disorganised capitalism, based on studies of five advanced industrial societies, they stress the significance of a new service class and its dislocating effect on the relationship between capital and labour.[4]

This service class, as its name suggests, works at the behest of those with established power largely by delineating the form and status of, and controlling access to, credentials which legitimate recruitment to institutionalised positions of trust and authority. Although the form of this new class varied among the five societies studied, in all of them it has substantially increased its powers in the second half of the twentieth century with the consequence that 'Knowledge has been significantly appropriated ... within the institutions of science, the professions, and education' (1987, p. 194). The power of those who control this knowledge is legit-imated and underwritten, much as Douglas and Isherwood have suggested, by discourses of technical rationality which weaken the cultural autonomy of the working class.

The political and institutional consequences of these structural changes have generated transformations that 'assume ... a fragmentation of working-class collective identity' (Lash and Urry 1987, p. 285), but it should not be assumed that the service class has an homogeneous cultural identity. They suggest, for example, that there will be divisions between distinctive sectional interests and in particular between those working in the public or private sectors. The disorganisation of capitalism will therefore have the consequence of a complementary disorganisation of culture with many established cultural forms being subverted or substantially transformed. Lash and Urry suggest that the political economy of capitalist disorganisation is embedded in what they call 'a *cultural* substrate. We think further that the contemporary cultural substrate bears certain features that can best be understood under the rubric of "postmodernism" ' (1987, p. 286; emphasis in original).

Lash and Urry are in this work significantly advancing any discussion of the changing powers and functions of the intelligentsia that has been a recurrent theme in theorising symbolic capital. In order to set out their approach it seems to me consistently appropriate that they have turned to Bourdieu's notions of symbolic capital and the habitus. Based on this theoretical resource they are able to illuminate why distinctive class fractions, particularly within the developing service class, will be drawn to the adoption of postmodern tastes and lifestyles as a source of legitimating images. In their subsequent book (1994) Lash and Urry are less concerned with the dynamics of structural disorganisation than with the implications of the impetus towards postmodern styles and goods that structural change generates (and is in turn intensified by). For now, I will not attempt to briefly summarise complex arguments, but I do want to note a central aspect of their approach. This grows out of their understanding of the increasing significance of symbolic capital and has major implications for our understanding of lifestyles in contemporary social order.

The argument is summarised in their claim 'that the sort of "economies of signs and space" that became pervasive in the wake of organized capitalism do not just lead to increasing meaninglessness, homegenization, abstraction, anomie and the destruction of the subject' (1994, p. 3). In other words, that some form of creative autonomy for social actors is still (or perhaps even more) possible in disorganised capitalism. A mode of creativity that is essentially grounded in increasing reflexivity and in particular in the vastly increased spaces opened up for aesthetic reflexivity: 'Aesthetic reflexivity is the very stuff of post-organized capitalist economies of signs and space' (1994, p. 59). Once again, then, we find that the notion of reflexivity is being made a key conceptual resource with which to understand the lifestyle commitments of consumer culture. Lash and Urry are concerned to demonstrate historic connections between social change and new forms of subjectivity and social affiliations: 'There are also many positive life spaces opened by the new socio-structural arrangements, in particular space for an increasing reflexivity of subjects' (1994, p. 54).

They are concerned to emphasise forms of action which develop in particular social circumstances. They use reflexivity to mean ways of acting that are informed by a consciousness of the self that acts by that actor – and therefore ways of acting that are imbued with personal meaning:

> If ideal-typically we can distinguish between traditional and reflexive action, the latter involves a rather larger role for agency than the former. It opens up a greater choice between alternative means, ends, conditions and legitimations of action. . . . And this involves a significant identity risk.
>
> (1994, p. 50)

It is in these ways that we can see how their use of reflexivity chimes with the emphasis on creativity autonomy that I have indicated that they see surviving in postmodern culture. It is further consistent with this approach that aesthetic reflexivity is understood to involve self-conscious interpretation of symbolic or semiotic signifying practices in particular.

If this particular mode of reflexivity is given greater weight in the changes of postmodernism it is because it encourages and is articulated in 'design-intensivity [which] is embodied in the "expressive component" of goods and services, a component having significance from the goods of the culture industries to the "managed heart" of flight attendants' (1994, p. 6). The more general significance of increased importance being attached to aesthetic matters both in everyday life and in the delineation of structural concerns is two-fold. First, to suggest an intrinsic connection between lifestyle practice and personal identity (an idea that I will develop in the next chapter); and, second, to suggest that the self-conscious aestheticism of the dandy is likely to be no longer restricted to avant-garde elites but becomes part of a more widespread aestheticisation of everyday life (an idea proposed in Featherstone 1991 and developed in the last part of the book).

NOTES

1 And both interestingly have been influenced by the studies of Basil Bernstein linking symbolic codes and socio-structural divisions, see Bernstein (1971).

2 Fowler makes this point by summarising Bourdieu's belief as being that 'Sociology must be the science which demystifies culture, just as Marx set out to show that the root of all social criticism is the criticism of religion' (1994, p. 129).

3 Reminding us that despite the prevalent tone of hostility to the privileges of the French upper classes in Bourdieu there are also persistent reminders of Parisian intellectual contempt for middle-brow taste (more generally see Rigby 1991).

4 A collection of papers also concerned with 'the new middle classes', their social bases and their culture (although with a more historical perspective than Lash and Urry) has been edited by Vidich (1995).

6
Symbolic process

In the two preceding chapters I have reviewed theoretical work relevant to rapidly increasing popular concern with ideas of life-styles. I have used a theme of symbolism throughout because the changes that I am concerned with are focused by the changing meanings and significance of the goods and services of everyday life. In this way, then, these goods and services are being treated as symbols of attitudes and expectations that constitute a distinctive form of life. Of course not every theorist who has written about these changes has used notions of symbolism or signification in the same sort of way. I have therefore suggested two groups of approach so far, the first focusing on structures of symbolic exchange, while the second focuses on the ways in which expertise in using different forms of symbolism is equivalent to mastery of modes of capital; thus enhancing our understanding of the dynamics of contemporary social structure.

Common to the accounts cited in both groups has, however, been a realisation that the symbolic relationship – that is, the tie that links a symbol to its referent and thus generates its meaning – is for a variety of reasons becoming in post-industrial societies increasingly arbitrary and unstable. It is in reaction to this latter theme that a further group of theorists has been led to emphasise the dynamic processes through which symbolic meanings are built into the structures and forms of everyday life. I will therefore devote a third chapter to briefly characterising some ideas in which, in quite diverse ways, the processual or dynamic dimensions of ways of using the symbolic materials of lifestyle practice have been emphasised.

I can begin by pointing to an aspect of Simmel's theorisation of modernity that resonates throughout the work I shall consider in this section. Simmel believed that it is possible in principle in all societies to make a distinction between the necessarily fragmented character of individual responses and imaginings and forms of concrete experience which stem from interaction with and intervention in an external world. The social reality of modernity, however, necessitates an engagement with its distinctive novelty. The character of modernity derives from the fact that experience of an external world is thrown into question: 'The external world becomes part of our internal world. In turn, the substantive element of the external world is reduced to a ceaseless flux. The fleeting, fragmentary and contradictory moments of our external life are all incorporated into our inner life' (Frisby 1985, p. 62). As Frisby goes on to emphasise, the problem this poses for social analysis is 'how is it possible to capture a fleeting, fragmentary and contradictory social reality that has been reduced to individual inner experience?' (p. 62).

In trying to consider how this is possible it is unsurprising to find that social theory, once again, should have turned to the analogy or model of language use. The reason is that language, as an institution that encompasses both the means of communication and the habits of speakers, combines in itself an order of stable practice and the variety of personal idiosyncrasy. If this is possible for human speech, and it clearly is, then it seems reasonable to hypothesise that the same sort of duality is true of social action – or more generally society – in more diffuse ways, in this way paralleling Simmel's notion of social life in general. I have also noted before that some thinkers have considered the possibility that all forms of social action will replicate a distinction between language (or competence) as the structured set of rules governing the possibilities of meaningful expression, and speech (or practice) as the infinite variety of more-or-less grammatical utterances that humans produce in everyday experience.

The trouble is that the language parallel, and the distinction between competence and performance in particular, left by itself generates a variety of further problems so that it fails as a model for social action. This is principally because the process (strategic flow of development) of any form of human interaction cannot be reduced to actors governed by structures of interpretation; and thus we find de Certeau introducing his study of the practices of everyday life by asserting that 'the act of speaking (with all the enuciative strategies that implies) is not reducible to a knowledge of the language' (1984, p. xiii). The alternative approach, and one that more appropriately responds to Simmel's challenge of how to capture a fleeting, fragmentary social reality, is to emphasise the creative or constitutive power of individual actors or actions.

I shall briefly amplify what is meant by de Certeau's phrase 'enunciative strategies' because for him it generates a distinctive approach to popular culture that has influenced other studies of lifestyles (more generally on de Certeau and attitudes to popular culture in French intellectual discourse see Rigby 1991). He goes on from the sentence I have just quoted to say that 'By adopting the point of view of enunciation . . . we privilege the act of speaking', and that there are four definitional characteristics of the speech act. These are: that speech is set within the field of a language system; that speakers appropriate language; that speech establishes a context of time and place; and that speech implies a necessary contract with 'an other' in a network of places and relations. This view of speech is obviously a dynamic stress on action as well as opening up the grounded-ness or what the ethno-methodologists have called the indexicality of speech.

Meaning is therefore something accomplished in engagement, a perspective that he develops in relation to reading, conversation and, importantly for the development of his approach, the manipulation of space. Meaning is not something 'there' in what we say or do or in the world around us to be appreciated correctly or not, but is something made in the politics of social practice. If this is valid, it is as true for social theory as for mundane experience and therefore he notes approvingly the Wittgensteinian idea that theory is always working at the limits of ordinary language. I hope it will be clear how his view of the relationship between speech and language creates a stress on the practice (that is the practical doing) of social action.

In this approach it is inadequate to merely chart the contours of lifestyle objects and activities: 'The thousands of people who buy a health magazine, the customers in a supermarket, the practitioners of urban space, the consumers of newspaper stories and legends – what do they make of what they "absorb", receive, and pay for?' (de Certeau 1984, p. 31). To make sense of the lexicon of users' practices we have to go beyond the model of speech to consider other 'logics' of social action and de Certeau suggests three – games, accounts, and tales and legends. In these unremarkable practices, actors in everyday life manipulate established forms of knowledge and discourse in order to appropriate the 'stuff' of mass society for idiosyncratic perspectives. In particular de Certeau stresses the embodiment of social life in established places must be counterposed to the creative organisation of experienced space; the latter being a way of using resources that rubs against the grain much as verbal humour exploits the ambiguities of language: 'Cross-cuts, fragments, cracks and lucky hits in the framework of a system . . . [such] . . . consumers' ways of operating are the practical equivalents of wit' (1984, p. 38).

It is in this context then that de Certeau stresses the significance of what he calls spatial practices (or, to point up the consistency with the original linguistic model, what he also refers to as pedestrian speech acts). The idea here is that as they move through established spatial and social order, actors are telling stories through their reinforcement and confirmation of local knowledges. The order created and imposed by established authorities will necessarily be involved in attempting to suppress these dialects of local meaning, but

> Things *extra* and *other* (details and excesses coming from elsewhere) insert themselves into the accepted framework, the imposed order . . . [so that] . . . The surface of this order is everwhere punched and torn open by ellipses, drifts, and leaks of meaning.
>
> (1984, p. 107).

The three themes that I particularly want to bring out of this account of the practices of everyday life are that: a) meaning is not fixed but is mobile and ever-changing (although with different rates of change between institutional sectors); b) meaning is inherently political because it is contested; and c) meaning is inscribed in our uses of objects, activities and places. We are then being firmly taken away from the structures of previous theoretical approaches, as becomes apparent when de Certeau argues that although Foucault and Bourdieu, in their different ways, seem to want to open a space for autonomous action – in practice they invert the logic of action and make it subject to their systematising discourse.

I have said that de Certeau's stress on the inherent instability of material meaning and the consequent politicisation of social meaning has been influential on contemporary theories of popular culture. One reason for this has been because the approach chimes well with other contemporary moves towards a more 'active' view of audience taste. One example of a way of using de Certeau's ideas can be seen in Fiske's radical re-writing of popular culture as permanent struggle: 'A text that is to be made into popular culture must, then, contain both the forces of domination and the opportunities to speak against them, the opportunities to oppose or evade them from subordinated, but not totally disempowered, positions' (Fiske 1989a, p. 25). Those cultural texts that have lost any opening to be re-appropriated by 'the people' have lost in Fiske's view any claim on popular status and, although such objects exist in general, 'What is distributed [by cultural industries] is not completed, finished goods, but the resources of everyday life, the raw material from which popular culture constitutes itself' (1989a, p. 35). He does, however, recognise that some of what he calls reading strategies by audiences may complacently collude with dominant meanings rather than introduce subversive alternatives.

There are obvious problems with this perspective, such as how the critic-analyst authenticates his/her interpretation of instances of subversive semiotics (see also Fiske 1989b), or indeed decides that audience understandings are insufficiently subversive. And curiously, although Fiske does emphasise the spatial locations within which his actors may practise their strategies of subversion, such as shopping malls, he is less sensitive to the personal politics of spatial practices, than, for example, Cohen and Taylor's (1993) account of different lifestyle practices as strategies of withdrawal and flight from the oppressive orthodoxies of conventional experience. In another strategy that also draws from de Certeau, Shields has suggested that lifestyles based on leisure spaces are inherently liminal – taking over Victor Turner's term for places that are outside normal social order – because in their marginality to dominant frameworks of meaning leisure spaces 'are open to the liminal chaos which places social arrangements in abeyance and suggests their arbitrary, cultural nature' (Shields 1992a, p. 8).

Shields continues to make two further points that are significant themes in the approach I call a concern with symbolic process. The first extends the idea that the meanings of activities are unstable and contradictory. If this is so it follows that the individual consumer is not necessarily a coherent subjectivity searching for particular rewards, but a more open-ended form of identity that is neither intrinsically rational or consistent. Shields (1992b and see also Langman 1992) in developing this idea is clearly extending the Simmelian theme of the fragmentation of reality in modernity, but not in horror so much as a gleeful celebration of a mode of subjectivity that is an alternative to the rational individual presupposed at the heart of bourgeois ideology: 'These *personae* are more like spiders at the centre of social and stylistic webs of their own making which extend the body in space, rather than the autonomous, disconnected and monadic ego-centred identities of bourgeois individuals' (Shields 1992a, p. 16).

The second theme is implicated in the previous quotation in that if we are re-thinking subjectivity, then the communities of sociable interaction are equivalently de-stabilised. No longer grounded in the institutionalised traditions of *gemeinschaft* communities, Shields envisages networks of solidarity dispersed over a multiplicity of sites and articulated in symbolic languages that are arbitrarily reflexive in ways that are impervious to ideology critique: 'Consumption for adornment, expression and group solidarity become not merely the means to a lifestyle, but the enactment of a lifestyle' (Shields 1992a, p. 16; see also Chaney 1994, Chapter 5). Here the significance of lifestyle in consumer culture is being envisaged to be more than the traditional views of either a distinctive mode of exploitation, or as new forms of structural status overlaying established class distinctions. Instead, we may have to re-think lifestyles as distinctive ways of being that call into question our understanding of the grounded embodiments of identity and community.

The challenge in these ideas is that the conventional relationship between symbol and reality is being questioned. Instead of symbols (such as lifestyle goods) just acting as counters or representations which refer to social facts, they are seen to constitute a distinctive social reality which requires new strategies of description and interpretation. It will be helpful at this stage to introduce some ideas of an author who embraced Simmel's difficulties in confronting a fragmentary social reality. Benjamin's major although uncompleted study of Parisian urban culture in the middle of the nineteenth century (partially published in English in 1973; although see also the commentaries and expositions in Frisby 1985, Chapter 4; Buck-Morss 1989; Tiedemann 1991) is neither a study of consumerism nor of lifestyles – except in his use of the *flâneur* as a social type that symbolizes some of the tensions of social change. It does, however, raise two themes that are fundamental to any account of the significance of lifestyles. The first is concerned with the character of urban culture and the second, more methodological, is concerned with interpreting the symbolism of collective dreams.

I have noted how increasing complexity of production processes allied with complementary specialisation in the provision of services has facilitated the growth of fashion in every sphere of life. Although insufficiently stressed so far, there must have been a spectacular growth in both the diversity of social contexts and the heterogeneity of social interaction. What this means is that in the process of modernity, the dominant tenor of social life had to shift from the stable intimacies of long association based in traditional communities to the fragmentary and perfunctory interactions of a community of strangers. Benjamin seizes on the new phenomenology of habitual crowd life in the nineteenth century – of course the mob has a much longer history but it is by definition an unusual and transitory phenomenon – as occasioning a distinct innovation in consciousness:

> For the crowd really is a spectacle in nature – if one may apply the term to social conditions. A street, a conflagration, or a traffic accident assemble people who are not defined along class lines. They present themselves as concrete gatherings, but socially they remain abstract – namely, in their isolated private interests.
>
> (Benjamin 1973, p. 62)

The significance of this innovation exists for Benjamin on a number of levels: it provides a new subject as well as a new audience for cultural producers; it necessitates new forms of social consciousness; and it provides a model for new relationships of personal and social experience. I will discuss aspects of each of these levels in slightly greater detail. It may seem that in doing so I have embarked upon a long and unnecessary digression. My reason is that in grasping the significance of the innovation of new forms of collective experience in modernity Benjamin is, almost in passing, telling us a great deal about a distinctive type of social life – something unique to modern experience. As lifestyles are an innovation of modernity, what is distinctive about the context in which they have developed will in turn illuminate lifestyles.

In relation to the theme of new subjects and audiences for culture Benjamin uses the poet Baudelaire as an emblematic figure through whom the anomic estrangement of literary consciousness can be read (see also Berman's use of Baudelaire counterposed to Marx as paradigmatic contrasts of modernity (1983, Chapters 2 and 3)). In a by now well-known move Benjamin seizes on Baudelaire's translation of a detective story by Edgar Allan Poe to function as a motif for the way a crowd generates anonymity and a mask behind which individuals are lost in their private deviance. Benjamin relates this generic innovation (the detective story) to other new cultural forms such as short gossipy news items in the press (known in French as *feuilletons*), cocktail hours and city gossip, the dioramas and other forms of visual spectacle, and photography, in particular its memorialisation of the ephemeral and the loss of what he called in another essay the aura of an art object (1970; more generally, it is significant that Benjamin read Simmel's essay on the characteristics of mental life in metropolitan culture (1971a) while working on his study of Paris).

The emerging metropolis (the apt characterisation of Benjamin's study as the 'prehistory of modernity' is Frisby's (1985)) therefore throws up cultural forms consonant with its new social formations, as well as generating new publics through the developing mass media. Moving to the second level, these publics, Benjamin suggests, do display new forms of social consciousness – particularly in their use of memory and traditions. The main instances he explores though are the transformations of commodities into a new state of collective dreaming exemplifed eventually in architectural and commercial innovations such as the new department stores. In fact, in the subtle dialectics of his critical imagination he uses mid-century Paris as a precursor of modernity and in much of his discussion concentrates on many of the vanishing echoes of the dying age. There is therefore a continual move between contrasting points in time in order to illuminate what is going to become dominant. Writing of new cultural forms he says:

> All these products are on the point of entering the market as commodities. But they still linger on the threshold. From this epoch spring the arcades and the interiors, the exhibition halls and the dioramas. They are residues of a dream-world. . . . Every epoch not only dreams the next, but while dreaming impels it towards wakefulness.
>
> (1973, p. 176)

Thus although the working title for Benjamin's study refers to the arcades (*Das Passagen-Werk*) they are significant less for what they are than in what their loss symbolises. In their glittering artificiality the exaggerated sociality of the arcades points forward to the all-pervasive transformation of social life into the pursuit of commodities. A pursuit which provides a form of intoxication or narcotic exhilaration formerly characteristic of crowds at markets, so that 'The commodity is bathed in a profane glow' (1973, p. 105). This glow masks its conditions of production and generates its own characteristic form of response: 'In the same measure as the expertness of a customer declines, the importance of his taste increases – both for him and for the manufacturer' (1973, p. 105). The crowd as a new form of urban spectacle is therefore complemented by new forms of participation and appropriation which are themselves characterised by spectacular show and dream-like illusion. We can now appreciate that Benjamin (anticipating Baudrillard) is leading us towards 'a theory of modern perception in which producer and consumer are alike afflicted by an illusory, false consciousness, a collective *unconscious* in which reality takes on the distorted form of a dream' (Buck-Morss 1986, p. 109).

When we turn to the third level, that of new social relations between individual and community, we find that again Benjamin uses an emblem of the preceding epoch to illuminate an emergent sociality. The *flâneur* is the best known of the marginal types, the category also includes whores, sandwich-men, collectors and other loiterers and outcasts (see Buck-Morss 1986 and 1989) who rub against the grain of the anonymity of the crowd.

The *flâneurs* were a form of dandy who devoted their lives to the social milieux of the arcades and were therefore privileged observers of social mores (Wolff (1990, Chapter 3) has pointed out that the lack of a female equivalent to the social type of the *flâneur* speaks to important absences in the discourse of modernity; on *flâneurs* in nineteenth-century Paris and their relevance to later social developments see the essays in Tester (1994). The privileged indolence of the *flâneur* could not survive the rude shocks of the bustle of the crowd – Benjamin writes of Baudelaire's fascination with and repulsion from the crowd – and yet as Buck-Morss argues: 'If the flâneur has disappeared as a specific figure, it is because the perceptive attitude which he embodied saturates modern existence, specifically, the society of mass consumption (and is the source of its illusions)' (1986, p. 104; ideas taken up in Part IV).

I think what Buck-Morss calls a perceptive attitude works in two closely-related ways that both exemplify the notion of reflexivity in modern society. One is a fundamentally ironic attitude in which the arbitrariness of any social arrangement and order is clearly grasped and enjoyed; while the second is a form of distancing so that the viewer refuses the complete seduction of collective dreams and retains a promise of subversion (Jenks (1995b) has provocatively used the idea of the *flâneur* as a model of sociological practice). Particularly in this second sense the pose of the *flâneur* offers a form of heroism that resonates throughout modernity. Benjamin quotes Baudelaire, acknowledging that 'For him dandyism was "the last shimmer of the heroic in times of decadence" ' (1973, p. 96). The development of the urban crowd was therefore for Benjamin both a form of incorporation into new forms of social order and the promise of the possibility of subversion that would eat at the entrails of bourgeois illusions.

Introducing my discussion of Benjamin I said that there were two themes in his study of nineteenth-century Paris that were fundamental to any understanding of modern life (and have therefore been taken up in subsequent theorisations of lifestyle practice). I have so far discussed the first theme, that concerned with urban culture, and will now turn to the second theme of the methodology of studying collective dreams. After all, as Frisby quotes Benjamin: 'Le monde domine par ses fantasmagories, c'est ... la modernité' (1985, p. 187). In his attempt to use the traces of a collective imagination of an era and a culture, Benjamin was necessarily stepping outside the bounds of conventional social theory and, more particularly, challenging the tenets of Marxist theory. Even within the Frankfurt School of critical theory reactions to his work were mixed. Cohen (1993) has suggested the generic title of Gothic Marxism to describe a critical practice that: values a culture's trivia and waste materials; that proposes a notion of critique close to psychoanalytic therapy; that seeks an emancipation of all the senses and particularly new ways of seeing; and that includes 'a valorization of the realm of culture's ghosts and phantasms as a significant and rich field of social production rather than a mirage to be dispelled' (p. 11).

The notion of collective dreams is clearly a puzzling one for conventional rationalist accounts of social action (the exemplary study of the flowering of the 'dream worlds' of mass consumption is Williams (1982)). Benjamin does not use dream in its literal sense of a mode of imagination that is 'only a dream' and which one contemplates when subsequently awake. Rather, collective dreams are in a dialectical relationship with conventional rationality and are only recoverable through dialectical critique: 'This is only possible if the world of phenomenal reality which leaves behind only traces of its origin is both structured and destructured' (Frisby 1985, p. 210). Grasping these traces is difficult and requires a rude awakening that interrupts, rather than is a return to, normality: 'This wresting of the fragment from its encrusted context requires a destructive intention in so far as the false continuum is reduced to rubble. Its significance is realized at that moment in which we confront it with surprise and shock' (1985, p. 216).

The distinctiveness of Benjamin's methodological proposal here is only really graspable when it is seen in relation to his ties to the Surrealist movement as well as his Marxism. Benjamin was active in Surrealist circles in the 1930s and although not an unqualified admirer of their ideas – indeed he criticised their use of dream materials precisely because they paid insufficient attention to the dialectic of awakening – his use of dream images as collective motifs is embedded in surrealism: 'It [Surrealism] can boast an extraordinary discovery. It was the first to perceive the revolutionary energies that appear in the "outmoded" ' (Benjamin quoted in Cohen 1993, p. 190). It is against this background that we can see how fragmentary refuse can take on the status of a motif: 'the paradigmatic surrealist act is not to hold a mirror up to the world. Rather the surrealist presents the world with a yielding substance where traces can be left' (Cohen 1993, p. 134).

Benjamin is therefore very far from a conventional study of lifestyles or even a theory of changing social order in which lifestyles become more important. He does, however, help us illuminate the broader context of consumer culture and what this entails in terms of how we might begin to formulate the meaning of personal and collective experience. He also shows the possibility of conceiving ways of representing the meaning of lifestyle practices that puts them in a more subtle dialectical or dialogic relationship of form and content: 'the theory is unique in its approach to modern society, because it takes mass culture seriously not merely as the source of the phantasmagoria of mass false consciousness, but as the source of collective energy to overcome it' (Buck-Morss 1989, p. 253).

A further aspect of Benjamin's significance for contemporary social theory should be mentioned. It has been well put by Buck-Morss: 'The *Passagen-Werk* suggests that it makes no sense to divide the era of capitalism into formalist "modernism" and historically eclectic "post-modernism" as these tendencies have been there from the start of industrial culture' (1989, p. 359). In part it makes no sense because Surrealist ideas anticipated so many themes in postmodern discourse, and to the extent that Benjamin used these ideas he calls conventional cultural periodisation into question. More importantly though it makes no sense because the 'problem' of modernity which Benjamin (and before him Simmel) very clearly identified is the appropriate representation of new social realities. This problem persists and is exaggerated in postmodern formulations – although in ways to which Benjamin might have been a reluctant or even unconscious witness.

Benjamin's possible reluctance stems from the way that the problem of appropriate representation of social reality can also be understood as a concern with the deracination (uprooting) of the intelligentsia in mass society. As a cultural formation the self-consciousness and identity of the intelligentsia has become one of the dominant themes of the discourses of modernity. This is because their numbers have been vastly expanded by the enormous growth in various modes of institutional expertise generated by the institutional proliferation of modernisation, and yet their social status has been made socially and culturally ambiguous by the very same processes of expansion.

In a series of books (see for example 1987, 1991 and 1992) Zygmunt Bauman has explored the complexities of modernity, its development and transcendence into postmodernity, and in particular the frequently agonised strains in intellectual discourse in attempting to acknowledge its limitations. Bauman emphasises the paradoxes of ambivalence for modern culture (see in particular 1991). These stem from the fact that ambivalence is a necessary consequence of any linguistic system. In naming the phenomena of everyday experience we attempt the impossible task of assigning them to classes and categories that are mutually exclusive and exhaustive. This ambition to conquer ambivalence is a defining characteristic of modernity. It leads to the devising of ever-more elaborate categories and lexicons of knowledge that will deny the potential chaos of human practice: 'The existence is modern in as far as it is guided by the urge of designing what otherwise would not be there: designing *of itself*' (Bauman 1991, p. 7). That this task is impossible is the awful consciousness of modernity, but in the hubris of seeking to deny this awareness new skills are invented: 'We can say that existence is modern in as far as it is effected by and sustained by *design, manipulation, management, engineering*' (1991, p. 7); and these are necessarily articulated by new dialects of expertise.

One way of reading the failure of attempts to devise a total national state, as in the 'communist bloc', is that these executive skills can not be exclusively appropriated by public bodies. It is part of the logic of citizenship and democratisation that they are privatised with further paradoxical consequences. The discourse of individuality encourages every member of society to value and develop their autonomy and yet the recognition of their individuality can only be communally determined. This is what Bauman calls the privatisation of ambivalence and generates a need for mediators or experts who are able 'to translate personal, subjective needs into questions which could be answered in the impartial and reliable . . . language of science, and to translate back the scientific verdict into practical advice for the layperson' (1991, p. 199). Bauman goes on to argue that the functional necessity of expertise in coping with ambivalence is generalised into more diffuse processes of reassurance, personal development and identity-making. Such expertise feeds upon itself and generates self-fulfilling prophecies which both, in terms of the provision of therapeutic services and the commodities of personal design, inform and validate local lifestyles.

Bauman is therefore arguing that the 'problem' of expertise is both created by the functional and institutional differentiation of modernisation and made insoluble by the same processes. The resultant crisis of authority in modernity is 'the stuff' of intellectual discourse, but spreads far beyond the local domains of the intelligentsia. In particular it can be seen to motivate *the investments in meaning and identity that constitute so much of everyday lifestyle practice*. If this analysis is persuasive then we could expect lifestyle sites (a phrase I develop and elucidate subsequently) to exemplify at least two contradictory tendencies. On the one hand the places where we seek lifestyle materials – literally shop for relevant commodities – could be expected to increasingly offer the reassurance of authority; while on the other hand the principle of ambivalence, as it is insoluble, is more likely to be increasingly accepted and become one of the thematic badges of lifestyle practice (on the necessity of anxiety in consumer culture, and more generally on the reflexivity of identities, see Warde (1994)).

In relation to the former point Bauman notes that, when hiding from ambivalence, 'The great American institution of the shopping mall offers . . . an escape from the messiness of the "real world" . . . a controlled, physically secure and spiritually secure environment for an alternative life-world' (1991, p. 226). In these temples to rationality the unreasonableness of personal hedonism can be indulged without guilt. While in relation to the second, contradictory, tendency, it also follows that if the stylistic heterogeneity of lifestyles displays, and indeed is premised upon, an increasing ambiguity of meaning, then lifestyles may be practical means of living with ambivalence. It further follows that, as one of the central claims for postmodern difference is a more general acceptance of the inevitability (and desireability) of ambivalence, so do 'The most conspicuous features of the postmodern condition: institutionalised pluralism, variety, contingency and ambivalence' (Bauman 1992, p. 187). It follows that an increasing significance of lifestyle practice is one of the preconditions of the cultural innovations of postmodernism – and again we find the idea being raised that the communities of new forms of sociality might be more profitably seen as looser neo-tribal forms of association (see Bauman 1991, Chapter 7; and 1992, Chapter 9).

The tension between these contradictory tendencies that I have inferred from Bauman's books has in fact a greater significance than I have so far indicated. This is that there is a necessary tension between a global rationality imposed by cultural corporations seeking economies of scale in the manufacture of taste, who are opposed by local knowledges which diffuse, subvert and appropriate commodities and services for 'irrational' styles. This tension is the contradictory face of postmodernism (Chaney 1994, Chapter 5). So many writers on contemporary post-industrial culture seem to emphasise one side or the other in the ways these processes are articulated, without appreciating that both are operating simultaneously. Both processes are therefore necessary presuppositions of any hermeneutic reading of lifestyle practices.

An adequate account of the nature of socio-cultural change in the later years of modernity has also been the theme of another sociologist writing in contemporary Britain (Giddens 1991, 1992 and 1994). Giddens has tackled the 'grand themes' of social theory, in particular what are often seen to be the competing emphases of either structure or agency (an analogous distinction to our old friends of language structure and personal speech), through a reconsideration of the character of modernity. In particular by insisting on the central significance of reflexive or recursive social processes. It is from a recognition of the importance of what he calls institutional reflexivity, as well as related processes of a separation of time and space and other disembedding mechanisms, in modernity that leads Giddens to the creativity of lifestyles: 'Modernity is a post-traditional order, in which the question, "How shall I live?" ... [and we know that in other places Giddens has added the related question "Who shall I be?"] ... has to be answered in day-to-day decisions about how to behave, what to wear and what to eat' (1991, p. 14); and subsequently: 'Put in another way, in the context of a post-traditional order, the self becomes a *reflexive project*' (1991, p. 32).

Some readers may be becoming impatient with a review of several authors who seem rather uneasily grouped together under a heading of symbolic process. The reason for choosing this heading is because it chimes with the headings for the other chapters of this part of the book, and because the idea of processual development is central to the analysis of symbolic meanings that runs through the approaches of the authors I have mentioned. But a more accurate title for this chapter would have involved a reference to the rather forbidding, although recurring, concept of reflexivity. I have at several points emphasised my view that lifestyles are reflexive concepts, meaning by this that there is a necessary open-endedness to the meanings of any lifestyle in context. (With the further implication that inescapable open-endedness precludes the possibility of adequate explanation of meaning by structural determinants.)

I hope that it is in the work that I have summarised in this chapter that the appropriateness – despite the diverse inflections – of the notion of reflexivity becomes clearer. This springs from the argument that the meanings of lifestyle practices are not primarily determined by 'forces' in the wider society (of whatever sort). It is rather that in the practical negotiation of distinctive life-worlds, the meanings of ways of using the symbolic resources of mass consumption are made into tangible objects and practices that are metaphors for themselves: ' "Reflexivity" here refers to the use of information about the conditions of activity as a means of regularly reordering and redefining what that activity is' (Giddens 1994, p. 86). For Giddens, then, the development of lifestyles and the structural changes of modernity are interlinked through institutional reflexivity: 'because of the "openness" of social life today, the pluralisation of contexts of action and the diversity of "authorities", lifestyle choice is increasingly important in the constitution of self-identity and daily activity' (1991, p. 5). To fully grasp this argument one has to appreciate that for Giddens self-identity is an embodied project, understood by individuals in terms of their own sense of, and ways of telling, personal identity and biography.

It will be apparent then that for Giddens lifestyles are more significant projects than characteristic leisure activities, and indeed he suggests that the notion of lifestyle has been corrupted by consumerism – although markets, particularly as they have become an ideological theme in neo-liberal politics, seem to offer freedom of choice and thus purport to promote individualism (some of the contradictions in the politics of consumer choice are explored in Keat *et al.* (1994)). Giddens argues that the commodification of selfhood, through genres of media narratives as much as marketing strategies, emphasises style at the expense of the investment of personal meaning. (Giddens's work is as he says primarily analytic rather than descriptive; for a more research-based report on how people understand the exploration of identity in the choices and tensions of mass consumption, see Lunt and Livingstone (1992).)

If lifestyles are understood as existential projects rather than the consequences of marketing programmes then they must have normative and political as well as aesthetic implications. Indeed, for Giddens a politics that flows from the significance of lifestyle in later modernity has to transform our understanding of emancipation. He therefore distinguishes between a tradition of emancipatory politics, in which activists seek to improve the organisation of collective life to enhance individual autonomy, and a more recent development of life politics. The latter do not 'primarily concern the conditions which liberate us in order to make choices: it is a politics *of* choice. While emancipatory politics is a politics of life chances, life politics is a politics of lifestyle' (1991, p. 214). Lifestyles in this view are processes of self-actualis-ation in which actors are reflexively concerned with how they should live in a context of global interdependence.

In his most recent book (in 1994) Giddens has explored in greater detail the possibilities for a radical life politics when a socialist programme of social engineering through the state seems exhausted, and traditional conservatism has been usurped by a neo-liberalism that privileges a competitive individualism above all other values. He outlines a framework for radical politics that is necessitated by and consistent with the familiar themes in his writing of globalisation, a post-traditional social order and a world of intensified reflexivity. The main points of this framework are: the need to repair social solidarities; the centrality of life politics;

a conception of generative politics; a stress on dialogic democracy; a concern to re-think the welfare state; and a recognition of the need to confront the role of violence. In this framework the second theme of life politics is concerned with disputes and struggles about how: 'we should live in a world where what used to be fixed by either nature or tradition is now subject to human decisions' (1994, p. 15); and subsequently: 'Life politics is a politics of identity as well as of choice' (1994, p. 91).

In developing his conception of life politics, and while looking in particular at the growth of concerns with ecological issues and thus the challenge green politics presents to conventional political polarities, Giddens argues for a recognition that the ecology of social action is as much concerned with individual experience as global threats: 'The body has had to be reflexively made ever since the combined influence of globalization and reflexivity did away with its acceptance as part of the given "landscape" of one's life' (1994, p. 224). It is in all the ways we routinely accept responsibilities for shaping and making and re-making our body, as with all other features of our lived world, that we can see connections between the marketing rhetoric of lifestyle choice – as for example between saturated and unsaturated fats – and the life politics of relating personal identity to ethical and aesthetic agendas.

Giddens provides a fitting conclusion to this chapter because in his account of social change lifestyles are seen as an important way of addressing aspects of the changing relations of individuality and community. In their quite different ways, the theorists I have discussed in these chapters have all pointed to distinctive features of the cultural formations of mass society. I believe that these inter-related accounts necessitate radical revisions in our conventional understanding of the social order of modernity. It may be that a re-formulated cultural history leads to the view that increasing commitments to lifestyle identifications is part of a process of passing beyond (to post?) modernity. Others may emphasise the logic of continuities in these changes. This need not detain at this stage. What is important is the recognition that the ways in which the symbolic resources developed in mass culture are appropriated as ways of delineating power and identity – the sorts of things we loosely refer to as lifestyle practices – are central to this revisionary thinking. Seizing this idea will enable us to grasp that the significance of lifestyles lies in how we think about the most fundamental themes of what it is to say that individuals are members of cultures.

Part III

Lifestyle sites and strategies

Introduction

In these chapters I shall explore some features of lifestyles in contemporary experience in order to see how this form of social association, and the socio-cultural changes I have been describing and explaining, can be assessed. I have chosen to give the general title of 'sites and strategies' to these chapters because I shall attempt to show that lifestyle practices tend to cluster around particular themes and concerns. This approach is quite different from trying to provide a typology of distinct lifestyles. The latter enterprise is unattractive for two reasons. First, even if accurate at the time of writing a contemporary typology quickly becomes out of date, and is more properly the valid concern of more ephemeral commentaries such as journalism. Second, a survey-based typology, such as that by Mitchell (1983), can describe social trends but not the reflexive re-working of identity in new modes of association. A typological approach cannot therefore address what it is that is significant about these social phenomena.

Instead, I shall argue that lifestyles tend to focus on certain social themes and display recurrent concerns. I summarise these focal themes by the heading sites and strategies. Sites, not because they are necessarily identifiable places in a physical environment, but because they are physical metaphors for the spaces that actors can appropriate or control. And strategies because, as we have seen, lifestyles are best understood as characteristic modes of social engagement, or narratives of identity, in which the actors concerned can embed the metaphors at hand. Sites and strategies then because lifestyles are creative projects, they are forms of enactment in which actors make judgements in delineating an environment.

Although I am suggesting that lifestyles are ways of doing things, the pairing of sites and strategies also implicitly grants a phenomenal or substantive form to lifestyles. This is because a site is necessarily extended in space (it can be distinguished by its boundaries), while a strategy is necessarily extended in time (it unfolds through the working out of purposes and intentions). It must, however, be remembered in relation to a social object such as a lifestyle that it is all too easy for us to think, as Shotter says, that with 'such things as "society", "the individual", "the person", "identity" . . . [etc.] . . . we all know perfectly well what "it" is that is represented by the concepts we use' (1993, pp. 198–9).

The alternative which I shall pursue in these chapters is to resist the temptation to presume a pre-existing social world. It follows that I further agree with Shotter that categories of social description such as lifestyles 'only "make sense" as they are developed within a discourse; [and] that such entities either have an imaginary component to them or are wholly or radically imaginary' (1993, p. 199). The social form of lifestyle does not then in my view represent a single type of entity but rather refers to a form of 'local knowledge' that we seek to disentangle. In the preface I described lifestyles as collections of things and processes that share a family likeness. What I mean now by local knowledge is the ways of framing relevant features that enables them to be seen as a family likeness (what Shotter calls a discourse). It is 'local' because it is shared as part of the distinctive skills that enable you to be who 'you' are.

Conceptualising a social object such as a lifestyle in terms of the twin dimensions of site and strategy I think makes it easier to see a useful distinction between way of life and lifestyle. I do not want to play with words here but I think the distinction is useful because it points to a distinctive type of sociality characteristic of lifestyles. A way of life is typically associated with a more-or-less stable community. It is displayed in features such as shared norms, rituals, patterns of social order and probably a distinctive dialect or speech community. A way of life is therefore close to one of Williams' definitions of culture as a form of life. Although in the looseness of ordinary speech we might refer to this way of life as a style of life I think this is misleading in the present context. Thus although Kephart's study (1982) of cultural minorities in the United States uses lifestyles as a central concept, the religious communities he describes are clearly instances of distinctive ways or forms of life.

Ways of life based on socio-structural forms such as occupation, gender, locality, ethnicity and age do not disappear because new forms of identification such as lifestyles become more significant. The ways of behaving associated with the conventional expectations for these structural categories are, however, interwoven with new patterns of choice (not least through the ways patterns of taste are used to establish and reinforce hierarchies of privilege and status). Zablocki and Kanter have suggested that 'life-style experimentation has taken place among people for whom occupational and economic role no longer provided a coherent set of values and for whom identity has come to be generated in the consumption rather than the production realm' (1976, p. 280); and while this is consistent with my approach, I would not like to restrict lifestyle innovations, as they do, to those caught up in the counter-cultural experiments of a particular era.

The focal concerns that I am describing in these chapters are some of the parameters within which choices are formulated and come to seem appropriate. Lifestyles are necessarily local forms of knowledge because they are always given specific identity through the particular context of established ways of life. The consequence of this analysis is though, as I have noted in my discussion of Bourdieu in Chapter 5, that conventional accounts of social culture are thrown into question. The idea that 'a' culture in societies of spectacle is a shared framework of norms, values and expectations is unsustainable because the ways of life exemplifying this framework are no longer stable and clear-cut. More significantly, culture has to be appreciated as a self-conscious repertoire of styles that are constantly being monitored and adapted rather than just the unconscious basis of social identity.

A lifestyle characterised by distinctive focal concerns with certain sites and strategies is not, then, necessarily an inclusive or embracing social group. Rather, lifestyles can co-exist, overlapping each other, expanding and contracting as social currents as successive fashions and inflections bring or lose those who feel some affinity with particular expectations for those focal concerns. For individuals lifestyles are likely to succeed each other in the course of biographical progression, but each is not necessarily mutually exclusive – and yet, again, there may be a master narrative as for the '60s generation' which is held to ground and inform successive stages of the life-course. To stress the self-conscious play of lifestyles is not to suggest that the actors concerned are fully aware of or in control of their actions – lifestyles can function as ideological filters much as other 'systems' of knowledge.[1]

I described lifestyles in their use as marketing categories in the third chapter as a form of social mapping. Picking this idea up again briefly, it is now more apparent that the terrain being mapped has none of the solidity and continuity of geological formations. The social groups identified or collected by their lifestyles are not distinct and stable entities. It is rather that the need for a vocabulary of lifestyles indicates a process of change towards the prevalence of more fluid and ambiguous structures of social identification. Personal experience tells us that certain objects, attitudes and styles become particularly significant as lifestyle icons in these shifting uncertainties. Thus a particular record, hat, colour, hairstyle or drink will function to unmistakably identify somebody in a particular taste culture. I shall in the following chapters illustrate the parameters of taste cultures through the use of perspectives of sites and strategies and their focal concerns such as: surfaces; selves; and sensibilities.

Baldly listed these are general concepts – what is their particular relevance to lifestyle practices? It would not be very helpful to try to summarise the arguments of the following sections. The general point is not that these themes have specific implications, but rather that as each theme will recur in a variety of ways in all lifestyles there is a continuity that recurs across the spectrum of social circumstance. I can illustrate how this works by noting an example that does not. Thus, one might say that the 'street' is a typical site for lifestyles, certainly if one recalls the model of those early versions of urban display – dandies and *flâneurs*. The point is not to deny the huge variety of forms of street life and their significance particularly for the lifestyles of those who feel marginalised and excluded. But in the context of suburban culture the street is not a crucial site – except perhaps as something to be driven along when it becomes a freeway. The street is not therefore a recurrent focus for lifestyles – it only becomes so in the context of other more general themes.

A focus such as a sense of self or a perceived sensibility recurs across the range of lifestyles in post-industrial societies for reasons that I set out in the following sections. Inevitably though a focus on a particular concern will be expressed through a variety of forms. I shall attempt to show what previously published social research can tell us about the cultural implications of changing forms of social identification. I will suggest that one way of summarising all these related changes in notions of culture and identity is to see lifestyles as re-formulating the boundaries between public and private spheres. Lifestyles were a product of the privatisation of communal life. A process that has been intensified by a move away from more public, communal, collective ways of participating in cultural occasions towards more private, personal modes of participation.

There are, however, further more wide-ranging implications which follow from pointing to social changes that differentiate lifestyles from ways of life. First, we have to reconsider the language of social description and explanation. By this I mean that traditional presuppositions about the solidity of significant phenomena such as classes and communities, and how these collective entities relate to or determine individual actions, are thrown into question. This is not because this type of entity has become less 'real' or powerful in processes of cultural change; they were always metaphorical fictions or analytic devices, but they seemed more persuasive when the terms of social identity were less malleable. The 'crisis' for social theory is then in how to adequately represent the building blocks of collective life.

This crisis is not confined to social theory but can also be seen to be undermining confidence in the rituals, ceremonies and figures that represent who 'we' are in different sorts of ways. And so a second implication of contemporary cultural change is that conventional presuppositions for the ways in which symbolic forms are grounded in social contexts are also de-stabilised. Symbolic forms such as religious beliefs, ideological orientations to responsibility and co-operation, and the rituals and ceremonials of institutionalised life – that is the forms and content of collective life (Chaney 1993) – are likely to be more self-consciously dramatised.

Third, these reconsiderations of how the terrain of cultural representation is to be explored now that we are less certain of it as the stable landscape of social facts jointly generate a further reconsideration of the analytic warrant of theoretical interpretation. On what basis can the social theorist claim the authority of expertise in relation to cultural forms that are continually being changed in use? These problematic implications stem from both an intellectual recognition that the categories of social description and interpretation are resources necessarily constituted in discourse (rather than responses to a pre-existing reality), and that in all sorts of ways the arbitrariness of social discourse is being reflexively exploited in everyday experience.

I have tried to show throughout the chapters so far that the changes in the organisation of social life represented by an increasing significance of lifestyles are part of what we mean by the development of modern life. I have also reiterated that these changes are associated with another feature of modern experience – an enormous growth in the size and range of institutional significance of a social stratum of experts or intellectuals. A central theme of the material I have surveyed has been that lifestyles focus on the exercise of skills and tastes that are particularly relevant to the expertise of the intelligentsia, and that lifestyle concerns have therefore been used as a display of distinctive forms of status. Further, that intellectuals will tend to invest lifestyle practices with normative significance – with both ethical and political significance. For example, strongly held religious beliefs and commitment to family values are likely to be symbolised by particular types of aesthetic choice, just as militant feminism is likely to be associated with particular ways of dressing, talking and leisure, etc.

It could, however, be argued that intellectual fascination with what is perceived as the self-conscious creativity of lifestyle choice blinds them (us) to the extent that the ability to exploit consumer discrimination is restricted to young upwardly mobile professionals. This type of social restriction would then be raised as a critical response to the significance of themes developed in this book. The criticism would be that a concern with lifestyle is exceptional rather than general, and is more particularly limited to those who can afford to be attracted to forms of social exhibitionism. This critique would therefore be that for social theorists to take notions of lifestyle and the illusions of capitalist marketing seriously is to replicate the mistakes of those social actors who seek individuality through forms of mass leisure. More particularly, it can be argued that an excessive concern with lifestyles is to treat too seriously the decadent illusions of new leisure classes (unlike Veblen 1924), and thereby misses the more general persistence of ways of life amongst more stable class communities.

It is true that lifestyle practices are, in important respects, displays of consumer competence – and thus recall Weber's distinction between hierarchies which develop from the basis of status differentials rather than class stratification which is based on processes of production. Lifestyles require therefore the resources, and a willingness, to be innovative with disposable income. And it further follows that it can be predicted that those social groups with low standards of living, such as the elderly or unemployed or with low disposable income through structures of employment, will in this respect be more likely to feel themselves excluded from pursuing the stylised chimera of lifestyle fashions. Correspondingly, we come back to studies such as those by Bourdieu and Savage which have suggested that lifestyle concerns are particularly associated with those who are relatively successful through their grasp of symbolic capital based on educational qualifications, and who therefore cluster around distinctive occupations and perhaps constitute a new service class (see also DiMaggio 1994). And yet the opportunities for creative innovation in remaking lives are not determined solely by economic resources.

This point is clarified by a further inflection which has been given to this critique by the debate about whether a feature of post-industrial economies has been the development of an underclass. Whether or not the process of de-industrialisation has actually been associated with the emergence of a permanently trapped group at the base of the social hierarchy, this group also being characterised by features such as irregular household formation and high levels of criminality, is not central to my concerns here. What is relevant is the rather mischevious suggestion that the lack of relevant skills amongst such a group and their consequent long-term exclusion from the production process means that they are the first exclusively consumption class of post-industrial society. That is, what differentiates this group is both their dependence upon and marginalisation from the markets of advertising, fashions and other leisure industries. The underclass in this view lack the autonomy to sustain a way of life but are at the same time permanently excluded from recruitment to any lifestyle fractions.

To some extent of course questions about whether the degree of disposable income determines who gets caught up in lifestyle concerns or not are empirical matters. And indeed the social distribution of lifestyle sites and strategies needs considerably more research. It seems to me, however, that an economistic critique takes the marketing of consumer culture too literally. To assume that lifestyles grow out of the strategies of marketing professionals is too crude, as the discussion in the previous chapter should have showed. It will be the argument of this chapter that lifestyles are important because they are practices imbued in their social contexts with aesthetic as well as structural significance. A sociology of taste should aspire to be able to respond to the distinctive exercise of discrimination which is the significance of its subject matter.

It is from this perspective that we can appreciate that a presumption that lifestyles are pre-eminently the hobbies of the elites and would-be elites misses the extent to which innovations in symbolic goods and services, as well as opportunities for leaders, performers and other modes of social mobility, can be and frequently are generated within disadvantaged groups. To make this argument is not to be complacent, nor does it miss the extent of exploitation frequently involved in the marketing of minority styles to mass audiences, but it does recognise that processes of exchange and innovation in relation to lifestyles as well as the more general relevance of these sites and strategies is by no means limited to economically privileged groups.

NOTES

1 Two points about this last phrase are: a) the recognition of the potentially ideological character of lifestyle discourse is itself an acknowledgement of the persistence of social structural affiliations although the character of these ideologies requires considerably more work; and b) I am using knowledge in relation to lifestyles in the loose sense of everyday understandings addressed by Berger and Luckmann (1967).

reason is of course that, as we have seen in the discussion of fashion in the previous chapters, taste is being exercised in relation to what is made available by industries of culture – whether it is cars, or clothes, or food, or even advice. There are, in the recurrent search for economies of scale, inevitable pressures to rationalisation in the organisation of markets by such industries. Ritzer, (1993) for example, has cleverly used Weberian theories of modernisation to argue that the rationalisation and standardisation of food retailing by a global corporation such as McDonalds, epitomises consumer illusions of convenience while being sold a degrading experience.

There is much that is very persuasive in Ritzer's critique (although it also seems to be more effective looking back than forward). We do have to recognise that surfaces are easy to manipulate so that options for choice can never be taken at face value. In discussing a theme of surfaces I am both pointing to certain characteristics in changing cultural forms, and I hope clarifying what I take to be some of the ambiguities in the creativity of a culture of spectacle. Thus I do not think that it is appropriate to condemn new forms of social identitification such as lifestyles, and the cultural context they imply, as just exploitative illusions. But I also recognise that while responding to the ways in which these are new forms of social identification, and their use in marking out new landscapes of affiliation and expression, we have constantly to attend to the regressive pressures to conformity and orthodoxy that frame the flickering lights of local particularity. I shall in this chapter discuss some of these contemporary cultural ambiguities by addressing the significance of surfaces for lifestyles.

Walking the streets of any modern locality one usually takes for granted the flickering surfaces of urban life. There is to begin with the kaleidoscopic swirl of the crowd. In the jumble of clothes, accoutrements and manners we absorb, but largely disattend, a stream of social signals. Those who are attractive, those who are interestingly different, those who are threatening and potentially dangerous, those who are likely to harass you either with a social survey or a request for money or sexual address, those who excite emotions of pity or awe – the crowd is an endless mix constantly being monitored by its members. What is involved in the tolerance and caution characteristic of a community of strangers is not centrally important now. What I want to point to is how little each of us usually needs in order to classify and negotiate others. Of course these initial classifications are superficial and generally based on stereotypes. They breed prejudice and in these ways do not facilitate communication, but they are an essential feature of the visual legibility of metropolitan life.

In addition to the surfaces of those people we mix with – both casually and fleetingly and those we meet regularly in work and leisure settings – our environment is full of other sorts of visual clues. These include advertising imagery, the signage of commercial and public buildings and the clutter of street furniture, litter and the iconography of public spaces. We can classify and try to order this heterogeneity of semiosis but the point is not how much 'information' there is in any particular setting, but how routinely it is monitored and relevant details appropriated. The density of metropolitan space does not have to be learnt through patient absorption but is available as gaudy spectacle – vulgar, jumbled, transitory. Above all, although there are other assaults on our senses such as through our hearing and sense of smell, the profusion of imagery I am trying to evoke is a visual spectacle. The combination of the inherent anonymity of urban crowds, allied with mass retailing, industries of mass leisure and entertainment and the provision of public information for those seeking guidance in alienating spaces all work to create an insistent chatter of visual imagery.

It is arguable that the epistemological rhetoric of European culture has been dependent upon visual metaphors since classical Greece (see for example Jenks (1995a); and Sennett's summary, 'the Greek word for "theory" is theoria, which means "look at", "seeing" or – in the modern usage that combines light with understanding – "illumination" ' (1991, p. 8)). What I want to develop now, however, is the more restricted argument that as urban life has become the determining precondition of everyday life for national culture in modernity, so visualisation has become the central resource for communicating and appropriating meaning. And flowing from this, to the extent that lifestyles are one of the main frameworks for organising and manipulating social identity, then lifestyles are primarily articulated through the constantly changing spectacle of surface appearances.

Complementing this perspective are two further implied points. The first is that the appearance of what is to be seen becomes of crucial importance because that is the primary source of meaning, and second, aware of the significance of appearance members of modern culture attach overwhelming importance to monitoring their own and those other appearances that they can control. In combination, these arguments can be summarised as saying that the surfaces of social phenomena are invested with particular significance, and therefore that matters of concern in lifestyle distinctions are likely to be focused on the manipulation and interpretation of surfaces.[1]

The reason why visualisation has come to dominate the hermeneutics of everyday life in metropolitan culture is that the landscape scale of the rapidly expanding cities of the nineteenth century meant that a communal cognitive order became largely unsustainable. Devising and utilising new ways of searching for visual intelligibility became necessary ways of coping with cognitive alienation. One is the way in which the city was no longer allowed to rest as an ad hoc accumulation of residences and functions in the nineteenth century. It was torn apart to create symbols of a new social order initially ushered in by new transport facilities, and consequentially those temples of secular progress, the railway termini. More generally, the growth of new public buildings in government, finance, education, health, commercial ventures and entertainments such as theatres were all part of the city being re-built as spectacular hubris (Olsen 1986). Most famously in Baron Haussman's boulevards in Paris, but on a lesser scale throughout Europe, the city was re-created as visual spectacle. In part to contribute to the invention of traditions that inaugurated new national rhetorics, and in part to create a utopian imagery for the spectacles of commerce, entertainment and government that embodied the paradoxes (in which the individual is both courted and atomised) of citizenship. In time, the idea that the city is a moral responsibility was professionalised by the invention of town planners and a whole new discipline of visual order (Watkin 1977).

A second way of searching for visual intelligibility was inaugurated through the proliferation of technologies of representation. It is well known that in the early years of the nineteenth century inventors in several countries were desperately seeking solutions to the difficulties of photography and thereby inaugurating the first mass medium of mass entertainment. It is less well-known that the camera as an impersonal medium of representation was part of a broader climate of entertainment through new media of pictorial representation. Dioramas, panoramas, magic lanterns and a myriad other new forms of entertainment initially grappled with urban chaos through providing technologies of synoptic representation.[2] As the century wore on the impossibility of a synoptic bird's-eye view of social life or urban topography became increasingly apparent, and visual technologies moved away from a search for inherent coherence towards new forms of representation through fragmentation and arbitrary conjunction. In the new visual language of the cinema being developed at the end of the century an iconography of modernity (and modernism) was being self-consciously invented.

Foucault's adoption of Bentham's invention of the panopticon (a prison in which all the inhabitants are continuously under visual surveillance) as an exemplary model of new disciplinary regimes of modernity is also well known (Foucault 1977). The appropriation of visual technology as a central mechanism of power is another dimension of the predominance of visualisation; it serves to remind us of the reciprocity of sight. Ways of seeing are also necessarily ways of being seen – an inescapability of observation that is unsurprisingly central to the fantasies of modernity.[3] I have noted in previous chapters how several theorists have used the metaphor of dreams, a visual mode of representation above all else, as a way of capturing the uncanny tenor of urban freedom and powerlessness. It also seems relevant that a new epistemology of self-discovery, brought into being under the aegis of medicine at the end of the nineteenth century, should privilege dreams as visual representations of traumatic themes. Although the practice of the new interpretive profession of psychoanalysis inaugurated the 'talking cure', its analytical metaphors were above all concerned with ways of seeing.

The predominance of vision as interpretive resource for modernity is therefore complex and can be seen (itself an unremarkable but telling metaphor) to be operating at a number of levels simultaneously. It is characteristic of this theme in contemporary culture that we have come to increasingly speak of public identities as 'images'. Thus both corporations and celebrities and other sorts of public figures such as politicians seek to manipulate their image in ways that are flattering and that avoid damaging publicity. It is commonplace to criticise such an emphasis upon image rather than substance as superficial, as indeed it is, but it clearly also points to the salience of metaphors of perception and indeed the inescapability of others' seeing in the practical business of fashioning a self. In a stress on the verisimilitude of appearance meaning is freed from an organic basis in what is being represented and becomes autonomous.

An analogy may help to clarify the drift of this argument. I have mentioned at several points in previous chapters the idea that in the consumer culture of modernity markets have become abstract. What this means is that the traditional form of a market was a framed space – often literally marked out by perimeters or within a specific building – within which commodities (potentially anything) were made available to be exchanged. In the institutions of modernity markets are less likely to be confined to interpersonal transactions within specified places but become more abstract metaphors for structures of social relationships (within some ideologies even being given trans-historical autonomy). I would like to suggest that the history of performance in modernity has followed an analogous path.

At the inception of modernity new publics sought entertainment and were to some degree reflexively constituted in the commercially very profitable audiences for a large number of new developments in theatrical entertainment. In these new theatres social and technological innovations combined to structure the form of performance to heighten theatrical illusion through intensifying the 'realism' of representation. Theatres remained, however, framed spaces within which conventions of performance governed meaning and underwrote criteria of value. In the course of the nineteenth century the logic of performance expectations led to the pictorial syntax of the cinema in which as I have said an arbitrary order of fragmentary images worked to heighten illusions of an autonomous reality.

The subsequent development of television and other technologies of pictorial representation have intensified and vastly expanded what Raymond Williams called the dramatisation of everyday life in the dramatised society (1975; see also the essays on public events in Garber *et al.* (1993), and Dayan and Katz (1992)). In this process drama has been uprooted from the framing conventions of theatricality and become both more pervasive and a more abstract language of performance (in this respect see Sennett's innovative arguments (1977) on the loss of civility in cultural formations that lack strict frames for theatrical performance; see also Meyrowitz on the loss of place in media culture (1985)). In a complementary process of architectural change there has been a move away from the use of classical motifs to display power and authority symbolically on public buildings, to an emphasis on surfaces of colour and texture that mimic the iconography of leisure and entertainment.

One effect of de-framing drama is to generate an explosion

of semiosis. The signs through which we communicate no longer have to be grounded in particular narrative conventions; freed, they can be organised in an infinite multiplicity of conjunctions that can, however, become institutionalised in their own arbitrary logics of association. Perhaps the most obvious display of the confusion and complexity of pictorial imagery in modernity, and a form that is irredeemably ephemeral, is the enormous profusion of advertisements. These are characteristically two-dimensional images, either single printed images on a page or a wall site such as an advertising hoarding or brief (typically thirty second) dramatisations interspersed through an evening's television or cinema presentation. In their transitory ubiquitousness these images are an incessant hectoring chorus running alongside the more instrumental activities of everyday life. I imagine it is because advertisements seem so desperately insistent on their presence and yet basically superfluous to, if not misleading about, the objects, organisations and activities they represent that they are so often resented as symbolising the illusions of consumer culture.

Adverts are illusory surfaces that gloss their subjects. The activities of producing, distributing and marketing advertisements are clearly a contemporary cultural industry but they are also dependent on other industries of mass communication and entertainment. In sociological commentaries on the cultural significance of the development of the advertising industry it has become attractive to seek to read adverts for their narrative content. This is because as any one advert is a fragmentary image it seems necessary to seek to discover ways of coding modes of representation; then through the use of these recurrent codes the analyst can hope to show ideological themes that are not apparent in single instances (thus Williamson 1978); or, indeed, show interesting differences in, for example, cultural presuppositions about gendered spheres (see Giaccardi 1995).

One of the most persuasive instances of critical reading has come in the way a number of studies have decoded the representations of gender in advertising narratives – that is by showing ways of representing power, spheres of competence and desirability that are so pervasive that they function as strategic rituals in everyday life (Goffman 1977). While these representational codes (which are often called languages) are clearly relevant to the marketing of forms of social identity, they do not seem to me to be the most significant feature of mass advertising. Rather, this is that advertising comes to institutionalise the ubiquitous use of imagery of style to communicate associations and sensibilities (Ewen 1990).

Of course, one should not write about mass advertising as a single homogeneous cultural form. Leiss *et al.* (1986) have usefully set out an historical framework within which changes in marketing strategies and modes of presentation over the past hundred years can be related. In relation to the latter modes of presentation they suggest a typology of four formats – product information, product image, personalised and lifestyle formats. Each has been successively dominant in turn, with the last becoming more common in the last twenty years. In lifestyle advertising 'people, products, and settings of consumption are harmonized around a unified impression' (Leiss *et al.* 1986, p. 210); and they go on to suggest that this unifying impression is more typically something 'appropriate to or typical of a social group or situation rather than use, satisfaction or utility' (p. 215). The argument is therefore that in the course of the development of mass advertising there has been a move away from a rationalist emphasis on functional satisfaction towards an emphasis on members of the audience's ability to create surfaces of meaning through the manipulation of association and evocation (see also Wernick (1991) on promotional culture).

This argument in turn contributes to a broader thesis that advertising, as it has developed and become such a constant feature of later modernity, has helped to formulate the cultural frames through which we articulate expectations for the materials of everyday life. Once again Leiss *et al.* suggest a developing sequence through the twentieth century of four stages of framing, which they label: idolatry (products presented as pure use value); iconology (products are given symbolic attributes); narcissism (products are personalised and judged interpersonally); and totemism, 'the product appears as a sign or indicator for a collectivity that is defined by its appearance and activities' (1986, p. 278). In this last, contemporary, mode of framing the emphasis on communication through surfaces becomes dominant, here: 'Consumption is meant to be a spectacle, a public enterprise: Product-related images ... [become] ... emblems for social collectivities, principally by means of their associations with lifestyles' (p. 295).

I have said that advertising has persistently irritated rationalists because it is deceptive, it seems likely to particularly hoodwink the gullible who should be protected and because it speaks to social meanings that distort reality.[4] More practically, advertising runs the risk of irritating its audiences through repetition and superficiality. It is unsurprising then that those whose occupation is the production and commissioning of advertisements should seek to generate novelty and interest through innovative narrative techniques. It is also consistent with the lifestyle trends in advertising, which as I have noted emphasise associations between attitudes and values in style and use in fragmentary references, that new narrative innovations use strategies 'such as hyperreal encoding, reflexivity and the use of hypersignifiers' (Goldman and Papson 1994, p. 24). What these technical terms mean is that 'Advertising in the age of hypersignification no longer tries to conceal the code – the meta-language – of the commodity aesthetic, but tries to turn the "code" itself into a Sign' (p. 25).

The various ways Goldman and Papson identify as the mechanisms of self-consciously explicit coding all serve to emphasise the artificiality of the appeal. The surface of the presentation becomes more important and in the emphasis on the mechanisms of presentation it seems as though the possibility of a meta-language is denied. Thus in the use of particular narrative devices – the inclusion of references to the process of production in the presented advertisement; the use of editing techniques which disrupt conventional narrative forms of continuity; inadequacies in camera control and other technical devices which usually denote documentary practice or other claims to non-commercial authenticity; and fragmentary incoherent discourses – contemporary advertising insists on both its arbitrariness and ultimate irrelevance and the inescapability of its presence. As Goldman and Papson point out, in Brechtian theatrical theory reflexive practices should serve to disrupt audience expectations and unmask ideological conventions, but in advertising reflexivity is being used to both ironicise and re-articulate discursive codes. The viewer is embarked upon a spiral of sophistication that invites playful responses: 'Cosmopolitan viewers can then consume the sign of someone conversant with both the content and the meta-language of ads' (p. 43).

The point of this brief review of theories of advertising style is that they illustrate the significance of surface imagery in contemporary culture. It will become apparent that a recurrent concern with authenticity runs through all these lifestyle themes, but it seems particularly salient to a theme of surfaces. This is largely because, while surface imagery has become pressingly significant for everyone, only particular social styles will pick up and exaggerate the 'play' of surfaces. There will therefore be a continuum of lifestyles from those in which the inauthenticity of surfaces is accepted, possibly with a shrug, to those who seek more 'authentic' forms of representation. It is not my intention here to attempt to evaluate lifestyle practices, but rather to point out how a focus for lifestyle concerns will be addressed in a variety of ways. This variety will map onto other contours of social location and identification so that definable sensibilities are readily apparent as a vocabulary of style that is itself a repertoire of surfaces.

It should also help us to see the relevance of an argument that a knowing ironicism is displayed in this form of spectacular dramaturgy. Irony in consumer culture, then, is the promise of glamour, in a multiplicity of forms, allied to a simultaneous awareness of the arbitrariness of the conventions and premises upon which judgements of glamour rest. I believe that it is consistent with this approach that a high and increasing proportion of lifestyle clothing is being produced that features the manufacturer's or sponsor's name on its surface. By lifestyle clothing I mean either conventional fashion wear such as shoes and jeans, or clothing that is tied to a specific type of leisure such as cycling, jogging, golf or a holiday company. Both types of clothing work as repertoires of signs that transcend their functional utility and define their wearers in particular images and associations.

I referred to manufacturer or sponsor above because it may be the company that actually makes the item, such as Levi-Strauss or Nike, or it may be a company primarily based in the production of other products that seeks via sponsorship to associate the clothing with those other products, such as Camel shoes or Calvin Klein glasses. In either case featuring the effective name on the surface of the garment may be advantageous to both manufacturer and customer. Of course one version of these advantages is that the manufacturer benefits from the free publicity of getting the customer to publicise the product on their behalf. This may be done through a relatively unobtrusive logo or through a large image of the corporate name.

The advantage for the customer is that they seek to display their taste through the expense or idiosyncrasy of the label they sport. This idea of acquiring status through the display of one's taste is not a new invention but traditionally it was done unobtrusively in ways that only other sophisticated customers could recognise. In the irony of spectacular taste such discretion is abandoned and a glorying in fashionable association becomes explicit. To see this as merely gullible may or may not be correct but is in any case missing the point. Putting the label, and in many cases a very large label, on the outside of one's clothes is to emphasise that it is their surface as fashionable gesture that is most important.

These points are just as relevant to wearing the badges of corporations or institutions, such as universities, that the wearer is unlikely to or indeed could not have attended. Other relevant examples are wearing insignia, badges, t-shirts, etc., which are part of a fellowship through either membership or association with certain attitudes, political movements such as environmental causes, and rock bands. It has been claimed that in the niceties of discriminating between bands a successful group will now expect to sell more t-shirts than CDs. The identity of the clothing through implicated advertising, other settings in which it is worn and other wearers all becomes a resource to be used straightforwardly or ironically by each new wearer.

It is possible then to trace how marketing resources such as labels, slogans and logos have been appropriated in lifestyles as an ambiguous play of surfaces. These are instances of the rhetoric of advertising being taken over into everyday life. Analogous processes of blurring distinctions between spheres have also meant that what I described above as innovatory narrative devices in contemporary advertising have been and are being taken over and used in other forms of visual entertainment. Thus the filming of performance and music videos designed to accompany music cuts on a channel such as MTV frequently uses the narrative rhetoric of lifestyle advertising (a televisual style that is carried over into their news as well as entertainment slots). I also described the devices of this rhetoric as a form of Brechtian deconstruction and it is again unsurprising to find many of these devices originally used in innovatory television drama such as *Hill Street Blues* being widely copied. Unsurprising because it is consistent with certain lifestyle trends that serials such as *Hill Street Blues* were explicitly designed to appeal to better-educated, youngish, professional audiences (Feuer *et al.* 1984).

I have tried to illustrate how an iconography, that is ways of picturing and seeing, new forms of social association in a culture of spectacle will generate complementary forms of ironic response in everyday use, but practical creativity is as I have said necessarily ambiguous. It is tempting to call glamourous environments transformations of reality but they are now so pervasive that it is hard to cling on to a sense of an original reality as a point of contrast. What is perhaps more relevant is that in the pursuit of glamour, consumer or entertainment environments seek to flatter customers through illusions of self. To the extent that they succeed customers are caught up in the languages of appearance used by mass culture industries; they are given illusions of distinctiveness in personal lifestyle that gloss the pressures to become trapped in surfaces over which they have no control.

One of the more extreme examples of this process is provided by the variety of DisneyWorlds that have been developed in several countries (Bryman 1995). The fantasy elements in the themed environments and rides clearly indicate that in certain respects these are utopian spaces 'outside' normality, but the worlds also contain idealisations of ideological heroes, national cultures and future environments (Rojek 1993). In these latter aspects then surface impressions are clearly being manipulated for ideological ends. More insidiously, though, DisneyWorlds provide excellent examples of the engineering of consent. In part because the surface of freedom in choosing what to do and how to do it is structured in ways that ensure compliance, and in part because the literal surfaces of the environment – walkways and how attendants must appear and behave for example – promote ideological messages about conformity and corporate control (these examples are spelt out in greater detail in Bryman (1995)). DisneyWorlds are therefore a form of entertainment that in their construction of glamour seek to prescribe a model lifestyle that denies the reflexivity of innovation.

Although I have recognised that DisneyWorlds are alternative realities, the principles of control they embody can also be detected in shopping centres, formula restaurants such as McDonalds, all those features of everyday life such as pubs given the surface of Victorianism, and other public spaces such as suburbs given illusory veneers of communal life. In all these instances customers are encountering engineered surfaces in which the semiotics of lifestyle practices are manipulated to counterfeit distinction. We should also remember how politicians, celebrities, performers and other public figures manipulate the surface of their image (their lifestyle) in order to engineer consent and support. In a subsequent chapter I will discuss some aspects of tourism as a form of mass entertainment because it is an important element in most lifestyle practices, and it further illuminates the contradictions between local expectations and the management of culture very well. There clearly is no easy way of resolving or determining the dynamics of these contradictions. The notion of surfaces is important as a site for lifestyle practices because it brings out the play of meanings in any negotiation of cultural forms. I will now look at the relationships between this sense of play and notions of social identity.

NOTES

1 There is a clear connection between my approach here and the theme, in theorising about postmodern culture, that an emphasis upon surfaces is one of its characteristics; but I do not want to develop it now as I as see the 'postmodern-ness' of lifestyles as essentially a digression at this stage.

2 I have written at greater length about the interdependence of theatrical innovations, new pictorial technologies and the structures of urban development in the nineteenth century in *Fictions of Collective Life* (1993, Chapter 3).

3 The oppressive power of visualisation – as a conjunction that is both seductive and threatening – has been experienced most directly by women and critically contested most effectively by feminist authors (see for example Kuhn (1985) and Wolff (1990)).

4 The difference between the first and the third of these objections is that the former concerns misleading claims about specific products while the latter concerns the ideological climate promoted by advertising discourse.

8

Selves

In the previous chapter I explored the theme of surfaces as a focal concern for lifestyles. In particular, I suggested a number of ways in which visual or spectacular show becomes more important in mass consumerism at the end of modernity. An emphasis upon surfaces is therefore addressing the importance of appearances – the ways in which objects, or places, or people present themselves or are presented. Because appearances are designed for a multiplicity of contexts or purposes they will become increasingly fragmentary and ephemeral. An emphasis upon surfaces presupposes that meanings (of objects, places or people) are not stable and are therefore dependent on the arbitrariness of perception and use.

There does also seem to have been a change in the later years of the modern era in the primary social base of identity. There is now a widespread feeling that whereas traditionally work or occupation determined social class and thus an individual's way of life, in the second half of the century leisure activities and/or consumer habits are being increasingly experienced by individuals as the basis of their social identity. If the process of consumption is a meaning-making enterprise, then who we are is reflexively being constituted in the process of the enterprise as much as what the enterprise is (Kellner (1992); see also the essays on 'spaces of self and society' in the same collection). It is part of what I mean by a notion of reflexivity that social entities such as actors and styles are given distinctive character by the manner of their performance (or enactment). It should not therefore be a surprise that issues of identity (both personal and collective) – its formation, stability, and change – have become a focal concern of lifestyle practices (for a more critical account of the necessity of destabilising identities in mass consumerism see Warde 1994).

I think it further follows that personal identities are made less stable and coherent in a culture in which the meanings of objects and practices are continually being re-created. The reason for asserting the necessity of the relationship is that if the meanings of things we are using or employing are unpredictable, then at least part of what they, the objects, will be taken to mean is dependent upon who is using them and how they are being used. And in the same way who we are – as active players in the game of consumption – is constructed and displayed through how we employ the resources of the game. It is this symbiotic relationship that has lead sociologists to believe (although it is an extremely tendentious belief) that they can 'read back' from patterns of consumption and leisure activities for answers to 'hugely significant questions about what we believe and think, how we arrive at our beliefs, what we do, and how our actions express particular beliefs or values' (Tomlinson 1990, p. 5; in different ways several of the essays in this collection touch on the malleability of identity in consumer culture; see also the much fuller discussion in Finkelstein (1991)).

In addition to this theoretical argument, it is appropriate to point to two further, more empirical, trends linking changes in consumer culture with notions of personal identity. The first can be summarised as a move away from more public, communal, collective ways of participating in cultural occasions towards more private, personal modes of participation – a process that can be described as decentring leisure. This shift in cultural style has in part been dependent upon technological developments, such as the video recorder and personal tape and CD players, which have made personal access to and control over performance ubiquitous. But the drive for technological innovation in this direction has been inspired by more general trends in the re-formulation of public and private spheres (a theme in recent work by Morley

(1992) and Silverstone (1994); see also the further discussion below).

The second change is related to the first and can be summarised as a fragmentation of the marketplace. I noted at several points in the previous chapter how the initial forms of consumerism that were built on mass production have been superseded by shifts in marketing away from broad-based audience categories towards increasingly specialised market niches (in contemporary journalism and television commentaries the development of lifestyle shopping is commonly equated with specialised marketing). This process again provides greater opportunities for individuals to invest their choices with personal significance so that a theme of personal development can be expressed in lifestyle choices. There are then a number of ways in which it is possible to see how notions of personal identity are likely to be de-stabilised in a culture of consumerism.

For the moment I shall continue to write of identity and the self as though they are the same thing. In due course at least the possibility of distinguishing between them will have to be considered, but for now it is easier to think of the terms as two aspects of a person's single, coherent individuality. We have seen that individuality or identity can be seen to be buried inside lifestyle choices. In the ways in which a lifestyle is drawn out or delineated, a particular version of the person making those choices is also being formulated. A story or a narrative is being told.[1] For conventional thought, though, a suggestion that individualities in contemporary society are becoming unstable so that they change and develop through a variety of appearances (and that we can be telling several stories, if not necessarily simultaneously, in continuous succession) is at least disturbing if not shocking.

I imagine that we all like to feel that who I am, or we are, is one thing we can assert with some confidence in an uncertain world – thus the drunk's affection for the song *My Way* as a defiant claim of integrity. And yet the presupposition of a distinct and unique individuality for each social body is a relatively modern belief. The discourses of individuality that are so fundamental to Western thought have not, however, existed for all time. In a book of essays on the social category of the person (Carrithers *et al.* 1985), a number of authors locate the transition to an assumption of universal individuality at the birth of modernity in European culture. It also follows, however, that if competitive individualistic notions of the self are historically and culturally specific, then these dominant conceptions of and expectations for the self can undergo further changes in the context of epochal cultural change.

It seems that there might a contradiction here between a widespread feeling that the coherent individuality of democratic citizenship is being de-stabilised by the blandishments of fashion and ephemeral display, and the intellectual argument that our notions of individuality are always and inherently relative. If the latter is true it seems difficult to see how we can explain how notions of the self and identity are changing, that is towards a more serial sense of re-creation through manipulating appearances, as a consequence of the development of a culture of mass consumerism. In the initial chapters I tried to show how a concern with fashion, taste and leisure can be seen to be dominating concerns throughout the modernising process. If this is so, it also follows that in certain respects the consumerist self, as something to be self-consciously shaped in the light of others' expectations, is also not a completely recent development but is a persistent theme in the modernising process. In his influential study of the discourses of civilised behaviour that can be found in books on manners from the early sixteenth to the nineteenth centuries, Elias (1978) sought to trace a new figuration of individuality in codes of interpersonal conduct.

What is particularly relevant about Elias's project for our present concerns is how he tries to show the emergence of new forms of self-consciousness in matters as 'trivial' as control of the body through regulation of its orifices both in eating, waste disposal and sexuality. Thus Elias's work suggests that new conceptions of the self were bound in with playful forms based on the *artificiality* of mannered conduct: 'The increased tendency of people to observe themselves and others is one sign of how the whole question of behavior is now [in the Renaissance] taking on a different character: people mould themselves and others more deliberately than in the Middle Ages' (Elias 1978, p. 79). While it would be anachronistic to call the manuals of advice on codes of civilised conduct that Elias studied templates for lifestyles, his work does suggest the significance of how, in the course of modernity, individuals have sought ways of discriminating between the more or less civilised and the more or less sophisticated.

Elias therefore opens up the possibility of studying histories of taste and manners as themes of changing lifestyles. Following this lead we can take advantage of histories of topics such as: the politeness of table manners (Visser 1991); types of food and the organisation of social rituals of eating (Mennell 1985); the self-restraint implicit in the calculated excess of the dandy (Moers 1978); and, perhaps above all, the dialectic between indulgence and control that is inherent in all conventions of sexual behaviour. It is intrinsically possible to study the ways different fashions in all these and other areas have diffused both across society and down through social hierarchies. In the processes of regulation of all these closely monitored spheres of social life, one can see how certain notions of desirable or civilised behaviour are being used to elaborate criteria of inclusion and exclusion: 'The terms good taste and bad taste . . . are crude ways of assigning value to things, but their validity derives only from the power and prestige of the social group that uses them . . . Taste is more to do with manners than *appearances*' (Bayley 1991, p. 71). The real paradox underlying processes of cultural change is that it is in the artificiality of social manners, that something as 'natural' as the self can become conscious and be articulated.

My more general thesis can then be formulated as a series of propositions. First, that the ways in which people experience and utilise their self-hood or individuality changes as part of more general cultural changes. Second, that the languages of individuality and identity will themselves be part of broader processes of delineating status formation and change (see for example Davidoff's (1973) study of elite society in the later nineteenth century). Third, that in the process of modernisation Western societies have developed particular forms of individuality that have been focused upon and expressed through spheres of social action – such as taste, manners and fashion – which are conventionally taken to be the province of lifestyle practices. And, finally, that these spheres of social action have become increasingly important in mapping social life as other forms of structural distinction have come to seem less dominant.

The conclusion of these propositions is that ways of managing the forms of identity will become increasingly central as ways of delineating distinctions between lifestyles. More particularly, I believe it follows that the idea of managing forms of identity will unproblematically translate into a set of concerns with regulating or disciplining an individual's body as the vehicle of self-hood, so that lifestyles can be expected to increasingly treat the management of the body as a focal concern: 'What is significant about contemporary society is the fact that the possibility of the body/self as a project is now open to a mass audience, being no longer

the goal or ideal of an elite court group or high bourgeois culture'
(Turner 1994, p. xiii; on the fashioning of the body as a display of
the self see Finkelstein (1991)). What I have called regulating or
disciplining the body, and Turner calls 'the body/self as a project',
both mean is that the more general issues of the recreation of the
self are expressed at least in part through the manipulation of
individual bodies as vehicles of lifestyle concern.

Why this should be so is I think fairly apparent, but I will
mention three points in order to develop the argument. The first
is that all human selves are necessarily embodied. If the dominant
discourse of the self in an era, that is the ways selves are discussed
and understood, changes then it must follow that expectations for
the material form, the body, of the self will also change. The second
point is closely related in that if self and body are symbiotically
associated, then it also follows that the form of the body will be
imbued with normative significance as a display of particular
values relating to the self – one can immediately think for example
of the emaciated body of the ascetic or the stigmata of the flagel-
lant. This in turn leading to a third point, which is associated with
the brief discussion of manners above, that the mode of deportment of the body will take on normative significance as an exemplification of particular modes of self-hood. Thus one thinks of the
way soldiers' erect bearing is taken to be an index of discipline
and manliness (and correspondingly in boy scout lore to sit in a
slumped position can be presumed to be an infallible sign of moral
depravity).

The further implication of stressing the interdependence of
selves and bodies is that if the self has become a central concern
of social theory in recent years, then it should be no surprise that
the body has also been 'discovered' as a topic for social theory
(Turner 1984; Shilling 1993). The contemporary history of theoretical discourse is not necessarily relevant in this context, but certain
aspects of the new interest in the body are relevant to lifestyle
practices. Turner has recently identified three themes in the literature on the social theory of the body (1994). First, the symbolic
significance of the body as a metaphor of social relationships – an
approach that has been particularly pursued in social and cultural
anthropology (Synott 1993). Writings in the second group have
focused on the discourses of gender, sex and sexuality (Bordo
1993). Third, as could be expected, there has been a tremendous
amount published which has been concerned with the medical
issues of sickness, disease and illness and particularly how these

categories are constructed. Each of these themes has been worked at in different modes of lifestyle practice, so that one can see here a dialogue between theory and the changing conventions of everyday life.

While it is less immediately apparent, there is a further level of interest in the 'construction' of the body. This is oriented to the ways in which our use of bodies articulates fundamental cultural assumptions about the inter-relationships of individual and community. Thus Turner argues that, while work on the social construction of the body has been immensely valuable, 'it fails to move beyond the notion of representation and social construction to a genuine understanding of social reciprocity' (1994, p. xi). I think that what Turner means by reciprocity here is a sense of the duality of the social body – both physical entity with characteristic structures and openings and cultural entity as a variety of modes of representation. Another way of characterising the reciprocity or duality of the social body is to see it as a symbolic form (O'Neill 1989), that is both representation of and a template for distinctive forms and values of sociality.

I can develop this idea by briefly citing a theme from Falk's book (1994 to which Turner's previously cited paper is a preface). Falk has proposed that in a highly integrated community with strong collective bonds: 'the more "open" is the body both to outside intervention and to a reciprocal relationship with its cultural/social context' (p. 12). In contrast, in a more open society with weaker communal bonds the more important it is to individual identity to guard the boundaries of the personal body. The distinction is captured by a contrast between the 'eating-community' of primitive societies, and the privatised forms of modernity where although people may eat together, as in a restaurant, they each eat their personal meals and share a community of discourse rather than a communion.[2]

Falk's proposal takes us back to the theme of privatisation in modern culture discussed above (as well as developing Elias's notion of figuration in conjunction with Douglas's and Bernstein's use of networks of group and grid). Now, however, the significance of changes in discourses of social identity is apparent as a more profound shift in sensibility: 'the great civilizing move from communion to communication characterizes not only meal rituals and foodways but the whole modern culture and the ways people relate to others, to themselves and ... to the objects of consumption' (Falk 1994, p. 36). Falk is therefore proposing that in the changing regulation of the body, and in particular the use of the mouth, we have a parable that illuminates the appeal of modern leisure: 'The very civilizing process that shifts the sensory emphasis from the contact senses to the distant senses creates a growing band of "spectator activities" ... from the theatre to spectator sport and the cinema' (1994, p. 64).

Falk's ideas here are exciting because they amplify the significance of embodiment for identity. In the process of communal privatisation, in addition to well-established themes in the discourse of lifestyles which stem from regulating bodies, such as increasing emphasis on diets and dieting, the importance of exercise in keeping young and 'trim', and the moral responsibility of guarding one's health, Falk brings out how the presentation of bodies (or selves in Goffman's famous title (1959)) represents particular forms of social identification and differentiation – that is, lifestyles.[3] The careful monitoring or regulating by each individual of their own and others' bodies (a form of representation that we take for granted) can then be read – at another level – as a story (or a fiction) of how we live as individuals in different modes of collective life.[4]

The cultural significance of the increasing concern with lifestyles in the twentieth century that is the occasion for this book can now be summarised. The significance is captured by an appreciation of how new symbolic forms of status (that is lifestyles) exemplify interdependent aspects of identity. That is, how social actors understand themselves as entities that are both part of new types of networks of 'we' and 'us', necessarily differentiated from 'they' and 'them', and as individual entities that simultaneously have a separate and unique existence. Lifestyles therefore provide a set of props for the person we would like to be that are comprehensible in the spaces and places we inhabit.

I said above that there were immediate advantages in not forcing a conceptual distinction between self and identity. I think the subsequent discussion of the dual aspects of identity has suggested that the interdependence between individual and social identities might now be re-phrased as a contrast between private and public spheres. The value of shifting to concepts of public and private is that they allow us to see that different levels of identity are distinguished by different patterns and types of role expectation and thereby 'embrace much of the entire contents of culture, society, personality and social character' (Bensman and Lilienfeld 1979, p. vii). It is not that one is a different sort of entity or being in public as opposed to private life, but rather that one is responding to different areas of concern, different types of sanction for inadequate performance, and differences in codes of appropriate expression, etc. Public and private spheres therefore pattern the whole of social life. They constitute frameworks which function as regions for different modes of social being.

The general significance of a terminology of public and private spheres for social theory is that it makes clear how different areas of life are inevitably in some sort of balance. Although I wrote above of the paradox that changes in forms of manners can facilitate the expression of the self, the paradox disappears if it is realised that a change in the character and rhetoric of one sphere will always have implications for an individual's expectations for the other. This does not preclude it being true in historical discourse that the balance between public and private spheres has frequently been seen to be unstable to the extent that they are in conflict. Thus a common theme in romantic thought has been the belief that the more formal obligations of public life are inauthentic, and that it is only in private experience that the individual can truly express their (or what is usually him-) self.

The boundary between public and private concerns, and their relative significance for individuals, will change historically (it is often argued that in postmodern society the spheres will be less sharply differentiated), but will also differ within a society during a particular era. In the process of modernisation the ways in which gender has been constructed as a mode of social identity have been particularly bound in with the delineation of public and private spheres (Davidoff and Hall 1987). Gendered differences in expectations for opportunities in public life, allied with differing investments in the search for appropriate means of personal expression, have and will mean that motivating concerns in lifestyle practices will take on quite different inflections between men and women within a common social framework.

The more particular implication of this sense of a shifting but necessary balance between public and private spheres for a study of lifestyles has two aspects. First, I hope that it further develops the approach above indicating how lifestyles work at negotiating the boundaries between the spheres. Although lifestyles are public practices – they are after all ways of discriminating social inclusion and exclusion – they are also invested with private meaning. The second aspect builds on this duality because an appreciation of the interdependence of the spheres is relevant to the meaning of certain lifestyle values. If the changing forms of public and private life open up a new way of writing a history of changing boundaries of self-hood (see for example Sennett 1977), they also allow new ways of approaching ideas such as intimacy and authenticity and how these values are articulated in lifestyles.

The intimate relationship is usually taken to be a privileged type of interaction which is more meaningful to the participants than relationships more thoroughly governed by public expectations. Intimacy in systems of social order structured by distinctions between public and private spheres will therefore be imbued with normative significance. This generalisation should give us pause though. Different ways of framing and bracketing intimacy are worked into what might appear common environments. Thus different modes of intimacy, as for example the contrast between a group of male colleagues who work together and may dress and talk in very similar ways, and an equivalently-aged group of women who above other similarities share a common concern with their female identity, will inform distinct but manifestly different lifestyle practices (the relevance of intimacy to lifestyle identifications has been explored most usefully by Giddens (1991, 1992)). It seems that the extent to which intimacy is offered or permitted is not just a function of a public/private contrast but is linked to more general ways in which the self is available as a topic for dialogue with others.

I mentioned above that intimacy is often bracketed with authenticity as a value of the private sphere. The reason is given in the idea that the self revealed in intimate settings is a truer, more authentic, version than that displayed on other more formal occasions. It is likely then that lifestyles that display a concern with particular forms of intimacy will also privilege what they see as authentic ways of acting or the value of more authentic objects. It is because in mass culture the impossible naivety of a claim to merely be who one really is can be taken for granted that there is an inherent indexicality (contextualisation) in social meaning. Individuals are faced with a choice between abandoning any attempt to control the presentation of self, or manipulating obvious semiotic clues to promote a particular style as characteristic of one's life (and thus part of who one is), or ironicising those clues in ways that suggest personal awareness of what they might mean so that intimate or casual viewers can appreciate the ambiguity of sense. At its most extreme a personal sense of conflict between public expectations and private desires can lead individuals to seek in their lifestyles ways of resisting or even fleeing normality – what Cohen and Taylor have explored as 'escape attempts' (1993).

Using consumption goods or lifestyle themes ironically does not mean that their ostensible meaning is called into question, merely that one is implying an awareness of what else is involved in having made those choices. Precisely, however, because the range of choices in how to dress, how to furnish your bedroom and what and how to serve your guests (to name some examples) is so enormous and continually changing through a play across different social strata that lifestyle magazines and other forms of journalistic commentary spring up to provide a discourse of style. This is not to say that this discourse determines the contours of lifestyle practices – rather that there is a necessary and continuous dialogue between local experience and the resources of mass culture industries. The scale of these industries means that local boundaries to experience are ambiguously dependent upon global cultures made available through ethnic restaurants and the other distribution networks and cultural forms of mass society.

With the development of lifestyle shops such as Habitat it has become relatively easy for mass customers to buy 'authentic' national crockery and other cooking aids, for example. This does not, however, exhaust the spiral of authenticity because it is always then possible for the self-consciously sophisticated to seek out goods that are not available through national retail chains (and thus avoid at least some of the stigma of commercialism). One way of doing this is is to go to ethnic districts of large cities and shop in retailers specialising for ethnic or national minorities, or to only buy from the country of origin. A further version of the latter strategy is to avoid as far as possible shopping in mass retail outlets and buy only 'craft' goods, that is things made individually with sometimes the aura of identifiable authored production. The difficulty with attempts to escape the uniformity of mass marketing is that they are necessarily dependent upon distinctions that can always be appropriated by mass culture industries.

The reason is that authenticity is not a quality with distinctive and unchanging properties. It is rather a judgement that changes with circumstances and contexts. It is obviously because lifestyles are frequently seen to be a matter of superficial appearances that some will seek to create their own lifestyle that focuses on more authentic concerns. These may be a concern to only eat food that is grown organically, or to resist conventional commitments to career paths, or to explore modes of sexual relationship that defy conventional gendered expectations or indeed that are not mono-gamous in heterosexual or homosexual couples. These instances, and many others that could have been used, show how frequently authenticity is a quality of lifestyle practice that seeks to contradict the production and marketing practices that have made lifestyles generally available.

But through a combination of new geographies of association and niche marketing suppliers of goods and services have proved able to meet contradictory expectations. Once again it is not that those involved are not making real choices, but that the play of surfaces creates distinctions that are matters of framing rather than qualitative difference. In the dramaturgy of appearance all actions are forms of performance. We come back to the point made above that taste is essentially a province of manners. Locked into the spiral of authenticity it may appear that differences are distinctions of degree whereas they are actually the concerns of style.

In this chapter I have been trying to show how a variety of forms of heightened consciousness of the self has been implicated in the development of consumer discourses throughout the process of modernisation. These forms of reflexive consciousness, typically expressed through an artificiality of conduct, deportment and the manners of contemporary civilisation, have intensified and become more pervasive in mass consumerism. I think this holds true despite the widely observed trend towards a relaxation or casualis-ation of codes of conduct in public places. This trend is not a rejection of social form, but rather an acknowledgement that the salience of intimacy and authenticity to the aesthetics of social action will be more generally recognised and shared as a focal concern of lifestyle practices.

To further illustrate and explain the point we can briefly turn to the variety of ways in which food has become a moral and aesthetic concern in contemporary culture. One of the most clearly apparent aspects of changing discourses about food comes in the shift from seeing food as a matter of practicality to being an aesthetic concern that is a display of social competence or even sophisticated taste. Hanke (1989) has charted how over a fifteen year period in one North American city, Philadelphia, lifestyle journalism became an increasingly significant feature of news-papers and magazines, and in particular how writing about food, cooking and restaurants took on a completely different character.

Once again we have here the development of a new (to Philadelphia) type of expertise, in which 'The diffusion of relatively esoteric knowledge' was both a response and helped to constitute 'a shift in the structure of culinary experiences and expectations, and the replacement of an ideology of "domesticity" with a new "urban" ideology of lifestyles, mobility, taste and pleasure' (Hanke 1989, p. 229).

Some other ways in which the social conventions governing the consumption of food and moral and aesthetic expectations about how much and what sorts of food are appropriate are, first, a further privatisation of eating towards what has been called serial grazing due to the breakdown of an established order to meal-times and conventional classifications of different types of food to be eaten at successive points in the day. Second, a vast increase in what I can call a disciplinary focus upon regulating the amount and types of food eaten, with a consequent industry of advice on the need for, and most effective modes of, dieting both associated in one way with pathologies of food abuse, particularly amongst young women (Turner 1984), and in another way with a discursive assumption that over-eating is a new sign of moral depravity. And, third, an enormous increase in moral discourses about the symbolic meanings of food (Mennell *et al.* 1992).

In relation to this third type of moral concern, an area that has generated a great deal of lifestyle attention, I can point to the complex of ideas and values associated with terms such as organic, natural and traditional. Common to these values are beliefs that the mass marketing of foods has led to bland, tasteless merchandise that not only exploits the raw material of animal products but also the producers of vegetable products, has contributed to the chemical destruction of the soil and other natural resources, and is harmful to consumers' health through over-use of pesticides, chemical ingredients and ingredients such as salts and fats. In addition to those who value more traditional styles of production and preparation of food items, there are consumers who seek assurance that their food has been produced in ways that are not exploitative of their environment. In these moral concerns with food it is unsurprising that vegetarianism, in a variety of guises, should be a growing aspect of lifestyle practice (Beardsworth and Keil 1992; Twigg 1983). Once again I should emphasise that to point to how a rhetoric of naturalism is being used to legitimate artificial constraints is not meant to be discrediting, but only clarifying the self-consciousness of lifestyle choices.

Investing food with moral significance is clearly not peculiar to consumer culture, indeed it must be one of the most basic modes of symbolism in human experience. What, however, is an innovation of modernity is the development of what I discussed at the end of the previous chapter as lifestyle politics. The morality of all the different aspects of producing, packaging and consuming food has become the basis of political movements – such as those who seek to promote animal welfare through to more general concerns with animal rights and environmental concerns (see for example Tester 1991). The politicisation of many different lifestyle concerns with the meaningfulness and validity of different ways of living has generated a large number of new social movements, in particular movements associated with new forms of spirituality. It is not appropriate to attempt to discuss or account for these movements in this context. What I have tried to do is to show how reflexive concerns with responsibility for the self have grown out of the new affiliations of lifestyle practice, and will necessarily inform the discourses of collective experience at the end of the era of modernity.

NOTES

1 Although I do not pursue the thought here, I shall come back to the idea that if identity is like a continuous story being told, at least in part, through different ways of living, then lifestyles can be thought of as genres – narrative modes – that collect themes and resources to ground particular stories.
2 We should bear in mind here Bayley's remark that 'Private dining-rooms are a theatre where individuals project their own taste and where everybody has a role' (1991, p. 196).
3 See for example Berking and Neckel (1993) on how the running of marathons in metropolitan centres can be seen as a way of staging a particular form of individuality.
4 I have explored an analogous theme in the privatisation of identity in relation to the cultural construction of honour in different settings (Chaney 1995).

9
Sensibilities

The idea that sensibilities are an important characteristic of lifestyles and should therefore be the subject of one of these chapters will not I imagine be controversial. It is apparent that a sense of a distinctive affinity in shared taste is what differentiates one lifestyle from another, and therefore that sensibilities are a recurrent focus of concern for all lifestyles. I have at several points already used an idea of sensibility as a way of referring to a perceived affiliation for an identifiable group with, for example, certain ideas, or values, or tastes in music, food or dress. A shared sensibility is not mandatory for all members, and may as we shall see vary between genders within a particular community so that sensibilities play across other more established ways of life. But clearly what gives the identification of a lifestyle a sense of affinity (or estrangement) is an assumption that certain predilections are self-evidently appropriate (or meaningless).

The theme of sensibility is then another aspect of delineating identities but here we are less concerned with personal than with communal identity. In the preceding chapter I tried to indicate how forms of identity are caught up in and become a focal concern for lifestyles. The initial premis of the discussion was that both personal and social identities have been de-stabilised and become ambiguous in a culture of mass consumerism. If this premis is correct, it will necessarily be reflected in and have implications for conventional expectations for sexual identities. This is because gender, as the cultural organisation of sexual difference, will provide a – if not the – major template for modes of social identity. A possible blurring of the force and significance of gendered identity will operate at a number of levels.

I will therefore begin a discussion of some aspects of how different sensibilities act as a form of collective identification by making some points about gender and sexuality before going on to discuss style and group identity in subcultures. Processes which have lead to the typicality of gendered characteristics being re-formulated will necessarily operate in a number of spheres. For example, we could expect that distinctive differences in ways of dressing, hair styles and use of adornments such as jewellery or personal cosmetics will all become less pronounced. Similarly, other typically gendered differences such as those that are reflected in the use of sports facilities, and the types of sports played, are changing for certain groups so that increasing numbers of women now demand access to sports clubs and facilities, and more generally other sorts of exercise, body-building and keep-fit courses and facilities. These trends, and the attitudes they articulate, are both a response to increasing concerns with lifestyles and underlie those concerns. I mean by this that changes in construction of gendered identities will constitute lifestyle differences, and they will in turn affect the sorts of things to which people will attach importance as expressing values that matter to them and that advertisers will be able to use these themes in lifestyle marketing.

Another aspect of changing gendered forms of identity will be a series of changes concerning those in same-sex relationships, those uncertain of their sexual orientation or who do not feel they have to decide within a binary choice,[1] and those who seek to change their sexual identity. In many cultures, traditionally, any blurring of conventional expectations for sexual affiliation and attraction has been met with extreme hostility. The sorts of trends I have been summarising so far should, therefore, be presumed to be based on a greater tolerance of sexual diversity[2] – as well as being caused to some extent by sexual minorities, and developments in feminist consciousness, refusing to accept repression and oppression by dominant moralities. The drift of this argument is towards emphasising that there are close connections between more extensive questioning of conventional forms of sexual distinction or difference, and the greater significance attached to lifestyle forms in late modernity.

The nature of these connections can be further clarified by making two more points about directions of influence or affiliation between changing forms of sexuality and lifestyles. The first is that those outside traditional forms of heterosexuality are likely to find the heightened dramaturgy of lifestyle practices suitable or comfortable in a number of ways. In relation to this first line of affiliation Bocock has argued that: 'It is one of the paradoxes of recent history that it seems to be the case that gay people are protected from being isolated and oppressed by developing a commercial, consumer-oriented, gay subculture' (1993, p. 104; even in context I am not clear why this is necessarily a paradox; see also Whittle 1994). The protection stems in Bocock's eyes from what is often a more generally exaggerated artificiality of consumer styles of leisure and fashion, etc.

This then leads on to the second line of affiliation which is that the cultural forms of consumer culture have been inflected or influenced by what I can call a camp sensibility. I can illustrate this by citing a paper by Savage (1990), in which he argues that the overt emphasis on sexuality in many forms of popular culture in Britain has disguised a more ambiguous and untramelled search for pleasure and self-expression focusing on the body. In the successive eras of 'pop' in Britain since 1950 Savage detects attitudes and values of homosexual milieux which could be packaged and popularised for mass audiences without acknowledging their antecedents, thus

> Androgyny – of an explicit and active kind – was the key sexuality of the mid-sixties. . . . The explicit blurring of the male and female into a different, 'third' sexuality represented a quantum leap from fifties timidities yet it originated from a similarly homosexual milieu and sensibility.
>
> (1990, p. 160; see also Chambers 1985)

While the evolution of style in relation to the delineation of sexualities is clearly a fascinating topic in its own right, this theme has also generated, in Savage's phrasing almost in passing, the idea that style can be taken as an expression of sensibility. What is meant by this idea is that style, from any area of taste, reflects or expresses in some way distinctive attitudes or values that are themselves part of a broader outlook or life-world. If styles can be read as, if you like, 'languages' of social identity then sensibilities, as the normative or aesthetic outlooks expressed through those languages, will inevitably act as central focal concerns for lifestyles. The implied sensibilities will be why lifestyles matter – why they (lifestyles) are treated as the iconography of community. To detect a shared sensibility is to propose a distinctive form of cultural affiliation. In the secular culture of modernity it may be that the values of a sensibility function to delineate the inscriptions of the sacred and the profane for common experience in the way that the values of a common religion once did.

I have suggested that lifestyles express, in part, the changing interdependence of individual and community. If new structures of social identification are being formulated, one can expect a theme of sensibility or taste to be used in a variety of ways to exemplify a perceived community or communal bond. General issues around the fate of communities in modernity are the perennial stuff of sociological debate and to pursue them here would be a digression.[3] One version of community in later modernity has, however, been more usually discussed under a heading of subcultures and is relevant here. This is because the idea of a subculture was invented to refer to a sense of perceived difference between the values and customs of an easily identifiable group and the practices of the conventional majority. Initially developed to describe and explain law-breaking and other forms of deviance by young people, the concept has been taken over to refer to forms of cultural dissidence and rebellion that characterise eras of modernity (Brake 1980, 1985).

The notion of a subculture privileges then the significance of style, fashion and the dramaturgy of identity in the play of cultural affiliation, but these elements are also importantly combined with the idea of sensibility as used above. That is, most writers seem to presume that in subcultural choices particular values and commitments are exemplified and made manifest: fashion becomes culture because it is almost a mythological enactment of strains and tensions in the structural context of the actors (Hall and Jefferson 1976). Thus, to choose one example from many possible, Hebdige accounts for the particular iconography of skinheads through the circumstances of working-class young men growing up in a world where traditional values have been rendered obsolete (Hebdige 1979; see also Robins and Cohen 1978). It is an important aspect of the tradition of subcultural analysis that the empirical focus has generally been directed at the street life of young people and in particular young men (for example Willis 1977; see also McRobbie 1980). The main reasons have been that the authors concerned have sought to emphasise the persistent relevance of theories of structural conflict to the idioms of consumer culture. (For an example of the same approach to a related field see Clarke and Critcher (1985) on theories of leisure.)

While this tradition has been valuable in refusing to see the languages of style as merely trivial or as the result of exploitation, it has been criticised for seeking inappropriate theoretical consciousness in actors' awareness of the cultural implications of lifestyle practices, and for presuming too great a coherence in the 'dominant' culture. Both types of criticism express feelings that the tradition of subcultural theorising has subordinated the ambiguities and inconsistencies of lived experience to the intellectualised categories of cultural theory. In subsequent publications authors who helped to formulate the subcultural perspective have significantly modified their views. For example, Hebdige (1988) has shown why he has moved away from the structural focus of subcultural theorising towards less determinist accounts of the meaning of style, and P. E. Willis (1991) has made more explicit the creative aspects of young people's use of consumer commodities. In order to develop our understanding of the significance of sensibility in communities such as subcultures, it will be helpful to briefly refer to three further studies.

I mentioned in the first chapter that Jenkins in his ethnographic study of working-class youth on a Belfast estate (1983) had used lifestyles rather than subculture partly in the light of the criticisms above and partly because he felt it necessary to bring out 'life-style differences both within and between classes; it is partly in this differentiation that a class-stratified society is socially constructed' (1983, p. 41). He identifies three lifestyles (in ascending order of 'respectability') for the young (predominantly men) on this estate: the lads; the ordinary kids; and the citizens. While the differences these terms represent can be traced back through other studies of working-class life, Jenkins is more concerned to show how ideal typical forms represent overlapping commitments and affiliations which nevertheless 'differ in important ways with respect to family background, inter-generational mobility, education and criminal records' (p. 67). Jenkins also suggests how these differing orientations to ambition, respectability and social order are expressed in related differences in leisure tastes, styles of clothing and a perceived need to distance themselves from their culture of origin.

Jenkins brings out how lifestyles in this particular cultural context can involve attitudes to the family, the self, masculinity and respectability as well as styles of consumption and leisure, etc. Another study which has used lifestyle instead of subculture, although not for the same theoretically developed reasons as Jenkins, is Hendry *et al.*'s (1993) study of leisure habits and values amongst Scottish young people. The study was primarily based on extensive survey research, although it did include a panel study component, and did not seek to identify lifestyles so much as assume that lifestyle differences would be expressed in patterns of leisure activities, involvement in sport and attitudes to 'healthy' or 'unhealthy' habits. While the authors do find that traditional structural variables, in particular social class, underlie and pattern much of the variation in actitivies that they chart, they also conclude 'that there were a variety of working class lifestyles; that there were a variety of middle class lifestyles; and that a few adolescent lifestyles cut across class boundaries and these were typically associated with youth-oriented culture' (1993, p. 174).

This broad-brush approach contrasts sharply with an early study by Willis (1978) in which he is trying to provide a reading of the stylistic homologies between particular cultural choices and clear subcultural/lifestyle affiliations. In this study Willis is concerned to explore how two distinctive cultural minorities – bikers and hippies – both constructed a coherent cultural world and used the sensibility displayed in the practices and choices of that world as a form of cultural politics, a distinctive form of creativity. This goal probably underlies what reads now as sometimes rather forced attempts to discover a coherence of subcultural style. Willis's account is, however, distinctively valuable for three reasons. First, he recognises the reflexive (although he does not use the term) form of any characterisation of cultural style through acknowledging the

difficulties in determining the structure and form, of the sensibility, values and attitudes ... because these things are never expressed directly but ... in a way which, I argue, helps to constitute the social group in the first place.

(1978, p. 192)

Second, and despite what I have just said, his account of implicit continuities in the styles of the material culture of these social groups' lifeworlds is still distinctively original. Thus, for example, his account of interdependencies for the bikers between: the integrity of objects, such as the feel of a motorbike; the attitudes, such as those to women and ethnic minorities; the tastes, in clothes and music, for example; and the values which inform an incoherent masculinity. The third value of this study is the insistence that 'We cannot . . . [or should not] . . . underestimate the importance of the struggle for an art in life . . . [through]. . . . Their very use of everyday objects and transformation of unnoticed habits' (1978, p. 172). Although these cultural minorities were deliberately provocative and often offensive to both dominant cultural values and organised political radicalism, his study is a classic recuperation of outsiders (what he celebrates as 'a profane culture') for his own values of emancipation.

Willis's book is a study of highly distinctive lifestyles. The members of these groups, self-consciously affiliating to esoteric formations, are clearly concerned to establish a marked degree of distinction between themselves and conventional style. What links these exclusive groups with the more pragmatic affiliations of wider lifestyle practices is, however, a common concern with style and in particular with the use of the insignia of fashion to delineate identification: 'styles of clothing have become part of our perceptual horizon; they mark out the boundaries of the acceptable. When we encounter others dressed in styles of their choice, we readily conclude that we are seeing their self-representations' (Finkelstein 1991, p. 115). In this emphasis upon fashion we are clearly going beyond the marketing strategies of haute couture, or even the ebb and flow of 'looks' which date eras.

I noted in previous chapters the importance attached to the mass institutionalisation of fashion by several theorists of modernity. Although fashion is often used to refer to changing styles of clothing, it has a more general relevance in relation to the social identifications of lifestyles as a name for the inherent malleability of taste. Fashion refers to all those ways of using goods, services and entertainments in which the social expectations governing individual choices regularly change, and are expected to change, both through time and within and between social groups. The prevalence of fashion literally displays the exercise of taste, an alignment to a sensibility. In the personal choices we make from public vocabularies (that is, fashions), we exercise and display sensibilities that inform and organise choice and taste. And for all these reasons fashion becomes more pervasive in a world in which surfaces are the primary means of apprehension.

I will suggest five aspects of the institutionalisation of mass fashion in modernity that cumulatively illuminate the significance of sensibilities. Fashion cannot exist without the existence of processes of production that make new social objects and activities available to target audiences, and that create related discourses of criticism, publicity and endorsement to explain and justify innovations. These processes of production and elucidation will obviously vary between different types of good, but to the extent that a feature of metropolitan society has been the provision of consumer goods to anonymous mass publics then the first aspect of fashion that is relevant is that it presumes the existence of consumer and entertainment industries. For goods, as a general name for all the variety of products of these industries, to be seen as appropriate and to excite interest and provoke desire they must exist at a level over and above their instrumental meaning. The second aspect of fashion is then that there is both a semiotic and a dramaturgy to fashionable display. The details of how goods are articulated and used are reflexively constitutive of their fashionable status.[4]

A particular aspect to what I have called the semiotic forms and dramaturgy of fashionable display is bound up with the conventions of delineating sexual difference and eroticism in different social contexts. Clearly clothes in particular, and all sorts of other aspects of taste in general, are highly gendered, and more specifically concerned with the communication of sexual attraction and an erotic frisson that must always nudge against the boundaries of 'respectability'. I noted at the beginning of this section that conventions of sexual identification and attraction have in certain respects become blurred in consumer culture, but in other important respects an encouragement of a pursuit of hedonism and bodily pleasures has heightened and made more pervasive a use of playful references to sexual nuance. In all these ways fashion encourages a self-consciousness,[5] a persistent reflexive awareness, about its own discriminations that necessarily privileges a third aspect of its significance – that fashion relativises taste.

It is in relation to this third aspect of relativising taste that fashion most clearly acts as a mechanism for inclusion and exclusion. While recognising that there are no absolute standards, local choices display affiliations and in that sense indicate the fourth aspect of fashion's significance – providing a bridge between social and personal identities: 'Fashion has become a major source of personal identification; in effect, this has meant that we have learned to value the image of how we appear to be, how we are styled. This is the fashioned self' (Finkelstein 1991, p. 146; see also Davis 1992). Too often, though, this aspect of identification has been treated as an index of the conforming acquiescence of mass men and women. Doubtless as part of the fears of the mediocrity of mass culture that have run through intellectual responses to popular culture, fashion has been condemned as a process of indoctrination, thereby missing the multiplicity of ways in which fashionable styles can be used to articulate dissidence as well as conformity (see in this respect Wilson 1985, especially Chapters 9–11). This fifth aspect of the significance of fashion, its potential as oppositional discourse, takes us back to the overlapping concerns of subcultures and lifestyles.

Fashion is therefore a name for social processes of use that change the meanings and significance of objects or activities. I can illustrate some of the implications of this approach by referring to a form of fashionable leisure. Modern tourism is selling a consumer good which is not so much a material good, although there may be incidental sales of tourist goods, but the use of places and facilities to generate extraordinary experiences. In consuming these goods the tourist is choosing to participate in a form of performance in which places are constituted for a variety of modes of appropriation. Urry has supplemented MacCanell's (1976) thesis of the quest for authenticity in tourism by distinguishing between types of touristic gaze, and by emphasising the development of post-tourists who know 'that they are a tourist and that tourism is a game, or rather a whole series of games with multiple texts and no single, authentic tourist experience' (Urry 1990b, p. 100). There is here a self-consciousness of performance which can be argued to be consistent with the reflexivity of lifestyle consciousness. Similarly, Munt has emphasised the development of ethical tourism which he argues 'is now a key characteristic of postmodern holidaying' (1994, p. 113), although he goes on to oppose the idea that such travelling can effectively resist 'McDonaldisation' and sees it rather as a differentiation between lifestyles.

Tourist activities are then clearly a significant feature of lifestyle differentiation. They display the exercise of a sensibility in relation to values I have already noted, such as a concern with authenticity, or narcissistic display or a delight in spectacular effects. The sensibilities displayed in these strategies for participation are analogous to the sorts of ways of classifying audiences used in marketing discourse that I noted in the third chapter, and also parallel the use of style in fashionable choices discussed above. Lash and Urry, for example, argue that 'if disorganized capitalism involves the dominance of non-material forms of production (especially images), then in many ways this is what tourism has always involved' (1994, p. 259). As the industry has become more all-encompassing, the tourist expectation of transformation has become less dependent on the uniqueness of the place and more on the ways in which it can be consumed as representation.[6]

I suggest that in the cultural reflexivity of later modernity the appeal of tourism is as part of more general processes through which reality is re-cast in spectacular form. The tourist seeks out appropriate places, images and idioms to exemplify a sensibility. As with other aspects of lifestyles, that which is sought are the materials for ways of living. Other cultures are pillaged in order to furnish a hyper-reality in which some of the discursive contradictions of consumer culture are magically resolved as spectacle. Mass fashion means that the cultural landscape is inherently unstable, a loss of any 'natural' continuity that might further suggest that there will be unstoppable progress towards an anarchy of taste. A regime of semiotic chaos that is a consequence of deterritorialisation or what, as we have seen, Baudrillard describes as a translation to hyper-reality.

And yet of course sensibilities are not as arbitrary and fickle as theory would dictate. In this respect it is helpful to note that a process of reterritorialisation has been suggested. This idea combines two themes, that while, first, 'the foundations of cultural territory ... are all open to new interpretations and understandings. ... Second ... culture is constantly reconstituted through social interaction' (Lull 1995, p. 159). It is in relation to these processes of reconstitution, of grounding continuities of taste in stylistic patterns that we can note some studies which have used a concept of taste culture to deal with the idea that there are cultural strata 'depending in part on social class position ... [describing] ... how people can be grouped according to their cultural preferences or "tastes" ' (Lull 1995, p. 192).

In these concluding paragraphs I want to change the direction of the perspective that I have been using to describe and explain themes in lifestyle practices. I have so far pointed to how personal tastes and choices often conform to fashions and styles that are associated with particular groups and thereby become icons of those groups' social and political attitudes and values. I have suggested that the practice of association displays a sensibility, an outlook, through which in that time and place the association comes to seem appropriate, natural, almost inevitable. It is in this way that the iconography of lifestyle often seems to have a taken-for-granted predictability in the heterogeneity of a community of strangers. In appreciating this process we have also to recognise, however, that individual social actors see the exercise of their taste as being part of who they are – it is a marking out of distinctive identity. On reflection they might grant that their choices will conform to the norms of 'people like us', but they will also cling on to the personal meanings of particular choices.

I suggest that a way of responding appropriately to the variety of personal meanings, and giving them due weight in any account of the sorts of things that lifestyles are, is to think of making a choice as being part of marking out the space that that person (the chooser) inhabits. To dress in a particular way, to choose particular sorts of chairs and pictures for where you live, to enjoy certain types of entertainment and to want to visit particular places are all part of constituting an ecology. They are all ways of delineating a sensibility in the terms of material culture, of imbuing the objects (goods) of cultural industries with symbolic meaning – what Csikszentmihalyi and Rochberg-Halton (1981) have called domestic symbols. More generally, I will argue that ecologies of community in mass consumer culture are another way of conceptualising what Silverstone (1994) has described as 'the suburbanisation of the public sphere' – that is that increasing investment in lifestyle distinctions is an inevitable corollary of life-worlds where the ecology of community is arbitrary and increasingly homogeneous.

One way in which we could embark on this project is to take seriously the ways people decorate and furnish their living space and more particularly what they hang on their walls (using that phrase broadly to include free-standing pictures and objects on shelves and other surfaces). Studies of what people mean by the objects they use, why they value them and how much importance they attach to the choices they make are surprisingly rare (for a more critical discussion of commodified practices see S. Willis 1991). After all, in choosing these things we are giving specific terms to the cultural form of the home, a 'Home, then, is a manifestation of an investment of meaning in space' (Silverstone 1994, p. 28).

This abstract version is made more concrete in the report of a BBC documentary about a number of people discussing their home furnishings (Parr and Barker 1992), when they note

> how infrequently people refer to strictly aesthetic matters. Instead their choices appear to be governed by a complex mix of public and private concerns: sentimentality, fantasy, personal belief, awareness of age and gender, susceptibility to fashion, and an often shifting self-image, combine with more public anxieties about class, social status and the approval of peers.
>
> (1992, p. 3)

These respondents, and we have no reason not to believe consumers more generally, are then always locating objects in networks of relationships and perceptions of relevant discourses. As I have noted before, the components of lifestyle practices are negotiating those points when personal meanings are necessarily given public form. Given the multiplicity of ways of framing objects, there may be both clear social patterns in types of concern and other cross-cutting distinctions within these patterns.

I can explain what I mean by noting an instance that amplifies the theme I have developed at several points about how gendered differences in expectations can be found to cut across common lifestyle patterns. The authors of the text accompanying the BBC documentary go on to report that 'In practically all relationships where divisions over taste were apparent, women were trying to achieve a *comfortable* look in the home, while their menfolk were more concerned about its overall *statement*' (1992, p. 4). A difference between seeing the home, necessarily straddling public and private boundaries, as looking outwards or inwards, and one that is consistent with Csikszentmihalyi and Rochberg-Halton's finding that when asked to nominate their most cherished object 'Males mention significantly more TV, stereo sets, sports equipment, vehicles and trophies. Females more often mention photographs, sculpture, plants, plates, glass, and textiles' (1981, p. 106).

These gendered differences in expectation operate within common class cultures although we also find clear differences in sensibility between classes. I have said that studies of the meaning of domestic things are surprisingly rare, but one example I have already cited is the study of eighty families in Chicago North

America, and their attitudes towards household goods, by Csiksz-entmihalyi and Rochberg-Halton (1981). Respondents were asked to nominate the objects in their home that were of special signifi-cance to them and also to briefly give some reasons for their choices. Even with a relatively small number of respondents this strategy generated a very large amount of interesting data. At this time I will only refer to their selection of visual art objects and photographs (26 per cent mentioned at least one visual object and 23 per cent mentioned at least one photograph as being of particular significance to them).

In general the authors found, as noted above in relation to the BBC survey, that 'the bulk of significations carried by visual "works of art" is not connected to aesthetic values and experiences but refers to the immediate life history of their owners' (1981, p. 65). This way of investing objects with meaning was even more pronounced in relation to photographs. Here the image was cher-ished exclusively because of the freight of personal association it carried, to such an extent that frequently when attempting to explain its significance respondents were reduced to tears. Particu-larly for older respondents 'photos serve the purpose of preserving the memory of personal ties. In their ability to arouse emotion there is no other object that can surpass them' (1981, p. 69). These visual objects are therefore embedded in networks of kinship and affiliation that give them private meaning, but they are also, particularly art objects, public phenomena – they can be accommo-dated in aesthetic and historical discourses independent of their local meanings.

I have concentrated on the selection of pictorial objects because it facilitates an interesting comparison with a British study of the objects people hang on their walls and the reasons they give for privileging these objects (Painter 1986). In this study the author was primarily concerned with the relationships between how members of the fine art community talk about the objects and images that they hang on their walls, with the comparable discourses of members of the general public. To this end Painter visited the homes of members of the fine art community living in or near to Newcastle-upon-Tyne, an industrial city in the north east of England, and 'ordinary' people from different social classes in the same city. Painter meticulously recorded all the objects hanging on the walls of the main living area of the household and informally interviewed residents on why it was there, what they thought of it, and to what extent they used aesthetic discourses to describe and evaluate objects.

Once again in summarising a wide-ranging study I can only pick out a very small detail to illustrate a more general point. I shall concentrate on social class differences in respondents' frameworks for responding to objects. In general, it seems that the people Painter interviewed fill out and clarify the distinction between social classes in access to and command of public discourses found in the Chicago study. In the middle-class areas 'Most people perceived their possessions in relation to a wider terrain of similar objects. Functional objects were situated within the world of antiques and pictures within the world of art. Their meanings were public' (Painter 1986, p. 367). This is not to say that everybody used these discourses comfortably or that it meant that their possessions were more meaningful than those owned by people from other social levels. It is rather that these aspects of their home have both personal connotations and reach out to other more impersonal frames of signification.

In contrast, for people living in working-class areas, objects 'were not situated within any larger publicly acknowledged framework ... [they] ... were often not on the walls as *things in themselves*, separate from other aspects of their owners' lives. Their meanings were often personal rather than public' (1986, p. 467). The objects that exemplify a home in this cultural context were then only comprehensible as part of networks of relationships – where and when they were acquired, who gave them or who was associated with their acquisition, and what has been implied in the occasions that the objects signify. Thus objects 'stood for people; they were points of reference in the passage of time in the lives of families; they were products of doing things' (1986, p. 469). To these ends a much more heterogeneous range of objects, often lacking any conventional qualities of aesthetic distinction but always imbued with a particular sense of what was implied in the relationship between object and individual, made up a very distinctive sense of the home.

Social class differences in attitudes towards decorative objects, taste cultures, are not in themselves lifestyles. But they do help to elucidate readily apparent sensibilities displayed in how people come to choose pictorial objects. Studies such as these help us to see how these objects and all the other goods of a material culture are hermeneutic texts embedded in larger, although frequently incoherent, narratives. I have suggested that we can conceptualise these narratives as ways of delineating spaces with which to organise everyday life. It will have become apparent from the studies cited in this chapter that, as a defining characteristic of communal identity, sensibilities are ambiguous entities. They are clearly important as interpretive resources, and yet such is the prejudice for determinist accounts in social theory that taste is almost always treated as a consequence or display of prior social conditions. How the tastes articulated in lifestyle identifications are institutionalised in specific circumstances is still a project for future studies. In the concluding part of the book I will briefly discuss the social aesthetics of lifestyle affiliations.

NOTES

1 The performance artist Jayne County, who has changed from her original identity of Wayne County, has summarised her position: 'I've stayed mainly as a girl, but it is very fluid. You don't have to be all one or the other. You have to find your level and my level is in the middle but relating more to the girl side. . . . Being just this or that is a form of brain-washing. You don't have to be rigid with your sexuality' (*Guardian* 17 June 1995, p. 28).

2 We should, however, recognise that a trend towards greater tolerance amongst the majority seems in modernity to carry with it a dark penumbra of intensified bigotry amongst significant minorities (Chaney 1994, Chapter 3).

3 Although I should note, and will return to this theme, that a dominant value in the suburban housing estates of mass metropolis is frequently a quest for the forms of authenticity that is echoed in more personal lifestyle practices (Chaney 1996).

4 While all the points I make here about the significance of fashion for modernity can also be used in relation to the significance of stardom, thereby suggesting a parallel that I do not have the space to pursue, these first two points are particularly illuminated by thinking of them in relation to the production and illumination of stars as transcendental figures (see Gledhill 1991).

5 The construction of gendered difference through a consciousness of being looked at has been a particularly important framework for female identity in consumer culture and thereby

differences in lifestyle expectations (see Gaines and Herzog 1990).

6 See also Urry's remarks: 'To the extent to which contemporary appropriations of the countryside involve treating it as a spectacle, even a "theme", this can be seen as a postmodern attitude to the countryside, to be contrasted with an approach which emphasises its "use" ' (1990b, p. 98).

Part IV

Conclusion

10

The aestheticisation of everyday life

In the several parts of this book I have explored the family likeness of lifestyles through their increasing significance, in the culture of post-industrial societies, as the most visible aspect of broader social and cultural changes in available forms of identity. To say this is to imply, and is meant to imply, that all the ways in which we identify ourselves and others are becoming more differentiated and that these forms of identity are also becoming less stable. And yet I have recognised at several points that processes of increasing mass suburbanisation, the increasing dominance of retailing by the anonymous illusions of shopping malls, and technologies of rationalisation such as that developed for the food industry by McDonald's seem to have diminished rather than enhanced cultural diversity. Or, more exactly, that cultural diversity has been fatally trivialised by the overarching sweep of a global 'normality'. These processes are also an inextricable part of the same social and economic changes that have been the context of lifestyle identifications. There is therefore an inescapable conflict between the diversity that I see as emancipating in contemporary culture and the pressures towards an effective homogeneity.

I have also chosen to address almost exclusively the goods and services employed in lifestyles as the material of symbolic practices. This has inevitably led to my focusing on how the meanings of these materials are constituted and, in turn, the constitutive and reflexive power of lifestyle practices. A major consequence of this perspective is that I have neglected the social consequences of new forms of material production, as in for example the environmentally destructive impacts of the widespread use of elaborate packaging or the effects of tourist development on local landscapes and cultures. To fail to stress these material implications is likely to imply a lack of concern, although this is not in fact the case. I should also note that increased concern with these issues has been and is a characteristic of lifestyle politics, in contrast to the themes of a more traditional radicalism based in a social structural politics.

There are evidently issues of the greatest importance involved in the cultural changes I have tried to elucidate in this book. I am aware that the approach I have adopted has meant a relative neglect of factors that might weigh heavily in an overall evaluation of the costs and benefits of consumerism, and has led to a possibly inappropriately positive account. I am sure, however, that a unidimensional evaluation will be simplistic. I have noted at several points that conventionally in sociological discourse the development of mass consumption has been seen as promoting inauthentic values and new forms of exploitation (for example, Haug 1986; Ewen 1990; and Cross 1993). It is possible that a general antipathy has, as might be expected of intellectuals, been rationalised into, in this case, a critique of capitalism which implies that in some pre- or post-capitalist cultures some more authentic way of life would become available. I know of nothing that persuades me that this view of the past is justified, and, as a hope for the future, the sense of authenticity that is being employed is at best extremely contentious.

In order to provide a more solid basis for further discussions of the ethics and aesthetics of lifestyle politics, it seems appropriate to conclude this review by briefly concentrating on the significance of design in the material culture of mass consumerism. The perspectives I have reviewed so far make culture and identity less coherent, less autonomous theoretical objects, but they leave the ways in which the one is embedded in the other ambiguous. I see the answer to questions about how we are to understand membership of contemporary culture as lying in the materiality of cultural forms. Being a member of a culture is having at hand the conventions of performance framing practical and character-istic ways of using objects and environments – that is distinctive forms of material culture (see Mukerji 1994). Each instance of a lifestyle is a way of telling a story, inflected by ways of life such as gender and class, that is a form of creative work. It is a way of redesigning material culture in infinite variety. A way of respond-ing to the 'presence' of several or a multiplicity of cultures in material objects and practices.

Clearly any study that is concerned with the social significance of how people use (consume) goods and services is caught up in what Appadurai has called 'the social life of things' (1986). Any study of material culture, in mass culture as in other social forma-tions, has to be based on ethnographic studies of the use of objects, innovations in trading practices, and the social roles of entrepren-eurial minorities, etc. At the same time we should not be guilty of the mistake of identifying 'culture with a set of objects, such as the arts in themselves, rather than seeing it as an *evaluation of the relationship through which objects are constituted as social forms*' (Miller 1991, p. 11; emphasis mine).

I have emphasised the phrase from Miller that I have quoted for two reasons. First, it contains a recommendation that we should never forget that cultural forms, such as lifestyles, are, in one sense, ethical and aesthetic projects – in their practice particular ways of understanding actors, their possibilities and their inter-relationships are recommended. Second, it implies that we should grasp the active reciprocity between actors and the world they inhabit – elements of that world are fashioned and shaped, are made meaningful, through institutionalisation and in their turn seem to necessitate particular forms of life. In this chapter I shall develop this theme that an active aesthetic is displayed in how we use (both playing with as well as using instrumentally), not just make, objects or elements of a material culture. I shall argue that aesthetic values are displayed in a reflexive awareness of design, meaning by that term for now a way of using objects that is aware of their associations and seeks to sustain an implied coherence, thereby 'claiming a perspicacity and subtlety in mass behaviour which is a far cry from the passivity, illusion and denigration implied in many self-proclaimed radical perspectives' (Miller 1991, p. 5).

The basis of a more active or creative sense of material culture can be initially found in the twin processes of what Miller calls recontextualisation and consumption work; both I think further aspects of the reterritorialisation discussed in the previous chapter. It is also relevant to recall that, when discussing the body as a vehicle of the self in Chapter 8, I cited Turner's point that we must go beyond constructionist accounts which treat the body as just an object (or vehicle) of discourse, and look at the reciprocity between the material entity (in that case the body) and its social being (Turner 1994). My account of a more active sense of material culture is then also directed towards elucidating the reciprocity of consumer goods. Of course, to theoretically describe several ways in which consumers can redesign their material culture does not mean that all consumers do so. Lifestyles will therefore vary in the extent to which particular practices display an aesthetic awareness.

What Miller means by recontextualisation is that all objects exist in hermeneutic as well as physical environments. These contexts are in general experience taken to be unproblematic, they are resources underlying the predictability of everyday life. The ways in which contexts overlap, are transformed in local experience and develop through time do not conform to structural principles (see the use of the examples of housing, scooters and fashion in Miller (1991, Chapter 9)). The argument is particularly relevant if we remember the previous discussion of how many of the goods of postmodern experience are themselves images: 'By employing the much-cited postmodern tactics of pastiche, irony, quotation, and juxtaposition, this kind of cultural politics engages directly with current images, forms, and ideas, subverting their intent and (re)appropriating their meanings' (Wolff 1990, p. 88).

The second term, consumption work, refers to the purposes of re-appropriation. Forms or types of objects are not more real, or better in other ways, because of the way, or the reasons for which, they have been made. What is more important is how they are used as tools – the work they are employed to accomplish:

> The authenticity of artefacts as culture derives, not from their relationship to some historical style or manufacturing process – in other words, there is no truth or falsity immanent in them – but rather from their active participation in a process of social self-creation.
>
> (Miller 1991, p. 215)

What is being made clear is the centrality of social aesthetics –

that is the ways in which we can evaluate the use by actors of the materials of their culture – in any critical account of changing patterns of social association.

I have said that a theme of design can help to explain the practice of social aesthetics in the material culture of everyday life. I shall develop this argument by a brief discussion of what we might mean by a notion of design. Although goods in all cultures have always had a design, in the sense that there is recognisable shape or form or pattern which clothes the functional structure, design as a self-conscious enterprise is one of the characteristics of modernity. What I mean by self-conscious enterprise is that it becomes a cultural possibility to appreciate, in both professional and lay discourse, the implications of, and rationale for, a distinction between form and function for any aspect of material culture. [1]

Given what I have said about consumerism as the motor of modernity in the first chapter, it will not be a surprise to read that the first significant innovations in the manipulation of design were as marketing strategies for mass audiences. In beginning his history of design in the late eighteenth century, Forty (1986) points to Wedgwood's use of neoclassical styles and images to boost his sales of pottery to a mass national market. There are, however, two other aspects to this example that are also central to any appreciation of the significance of design. The first is that the language of classicism that Wedgwood used was, beyond its role in ceramics, a broader ideological current for the social forces of modernising change. Second, the synthesising role of the designer in industrial production – as someone who had a clear sense of the relationship between form and function for the final product – facilitated an increasing division of labour that was an essential prerequisite of mass production.

The several dimensions of design throughout the history of the modern era have led to a constant vacillation in how influential actors have talked about its primary significance. I shall mention two of the contending perspectives as they can help to bring out the several meanings of design. The two perspectives I can summarise as functionalists and ideologists. The former recognise the functional necessity of design as a marketing strategy – it is in this sense an element in the production process which complements lifestyles as consumer strategies. Often derided as rather ephemeral and intrinsically feminine as opposed to the more masculinist technologies of real production, design in Britain has often been resented as the sort of thing that foreigners are likely to be good at (although art schools have been constantly urged to improve their training in these skills).

In contrast, ideologists have been less concerned with the practical rationales for design but have emphasised instead a guiding role for normative principles. Frequently avant garde, ideologists have argued that these principles should be used to inspire and evaluate designs as being more or less appropriate to the needs of modernity or the spirit of the age.[2] Although as I have said this perspective has been influenced by provocative interventions by figures as different as William Morris and the Arts and Crafts Movement in Britain, and the Constructivist Movement in revolutionary Russia, ideological design can be interpreted to exemplify both conservative and radical political goals. Ideological accounts of design have been particularly prevalent in architecture but can be generalised to include all aspects of the lived environment; see, for example, tasteful objects such as the Dieter Rams pocket calculator or Allesi coffee maker. (Both designs illustrated in Dormer (1993); on theories of architectural design in the first machine age see Banham (1960).)

Although within and between these perspectives there are clearly very different understandings of the central significance of design practice in the developing consumer culture of modernity, they have all in different ways accepted its importance in signalling and legitimating popular acceptance of constant innovation. Not just in terms of accepting new goods or facilities, such as the refrigerator, but in proposing redefinitions of household roles and constitutive imageries of modernity itself (important illustrations of this theme are developed in Forty's (1986) book). It is, however, this aspect of symbolising modernity that suggests a further reason for the inherent modernness of design concerns. I spoke above of the self-consciousness of design practice and another way of referring to this awareness of the cultural connotations of style is to describe it as reflexive. Designers' use of a language of style to ironically evoke or play with other contexts of use makes style a reflexive medium: a way of talking about itself and a way of talking about modernity.

The logic of a process in which the self-consciousness or reflexivity of design grows more important is that the goods of economic exchange begin to lose any foundation in intrinsic value or function (to return to a familiar theme). It seems that an inevitable consequence of a reflexivity of production is that style comes to supersede substance; style or design becomes more important than function. Of course what I have described as an inevitable consequence is affected by particular traditions and circumstances in each national context, but the drift towards the disorganised capitalism of what Lash and Urry have called 'economies of signs and spaces' (1994) is well established:

> Our claim is that ordinary manufacturing industry is becoming more and more like the production of culture. It is not that commodity manufacture provides the template, and culture follows, but that the culture industries have provided the template.
>
> (1994, p. 123)

In Falk's discussion of contemporary consumption (1994) he argues that if as consumers we are shifting from an appreciation of function to experience then the marketing of goods – particularly images – will change to representations of experience: 'What (all) the culture industries produce becomes increasingly, not like commodities but advertisements' (Lash and Urry, 1994 p. 138; more generally on the marketing of distinctiveness in cultural industries see Lury 1993, especially Part 1). Falk denies though that this process is just a consequence of manipulation by skilled strategists of public communication, but argues that it stems in large part from an individualisation of public forms. In the terms of this chapter the rhetoric or imagery of design has enabled the multiplicity of items constituting a material culture to be appropriated as personally meaningful: 'Mass culture transformed experiences into marketable products and advertising marketable products into representations, images and, with time, into experiences again' (Falk 1994, p. 178). Design therefore complements those other aspects of lifestyles I have already discussed as bridging distinctions between public and private spheres.

Summarising my approach to the significance of design so far, I have tried to make several points about how the development of design has been central to consumer culture. Thus, in addition to fostering a new history and aesthetic of style (represented in institutions such as the Design Museum in London),[3] a professionalisation of design has

- facilitated a rationalisation of production for mass markets;
- provided the material for a classification of 'looks' and eras

that has become the common sense of a widely-shared practical cultural competence;
• facilitated processes of market differentiation and new rhetorics of desire and personal involvement.

All these trends, and particularly the latter, have complemented and given substance to new patterns of association that we call lifestyles. The relevance of an increasing centrality and autonomy of design in marketing goods to the differentiation of the social forms of lifestyles will therefore be apparent.

It is, however, appropriate to recognise that because I can show that the increasing significance of design in the material culture of mass society has facilitated the elaboration of lifestyles, this does not mean that design is necessarily an important focus of lifestyle concern. My approach in this chapter has been constructed in order to show how a concern with design, as a focus for lifestyles, constitutes a sphere for the exercise of practical aesthetics. In order to do this I need to go beyond a concentration on a new mode of professional expertise, and the distinctive basis of an important fraction of the growing and changing service class, and do two things. The first is to bring out a version of design as a form of consumption work; and the second is to broaden the idea of consumption work from purchasing to using and evaluating material culture in ways that constitute local experience.

One of the most evocative figures in the history of modernity who has been committed above all else to living out the aesthetic principles of personal design, is the social type of the dandy. (Moers (1978) emphasises the literary as well as the social character of the phenomenon.) Pioneered at the end of the eighteenth century by Beau Brummell, a friend of the British Prince Regent, the initial style of the dandy established two defining characteristics that have run through the various exemplifications of lifestyles as cultural forms ever since. The first is a deliberate transcendence of established social hierarchy. Although Brummell's origins were not as obscure as he pretended, it was crucial to his emphasis on created rather than inherited distinction that the nobility should be terrified of the judgements of commoners. Moers points to Disraeli as someone from a stigmatised social background, a Jewish family, who used dandyism as an avenue of entry to elite society and established himself as a significant political figure (1978, Chapter 4; see also Finkelstein 1991, pp. 112–15).

The second is an unremitting refusal of any form of social

utility. Brummell and his friends prided themselves on the pursuit of style above function, and with an exaggerated concern with the minutest details of a dress code, the niceties of social form and an elaborate indifference to rational considerations. Brummell's era of dandyism therefore pioneered a new form of public display – whether strolling elegantly in a small number of streets or arcades, lounging in the window of a select club, or gracing exclusive social gatherings – in new types of public space. By these means the world of established privilege was opened up to the gaze and possible admiration of anonymous audiences.

Although dandies are conventionally associated with decadence, and in the sense of conspicuous idleness mentioned above this is right, in practice they emphasised restraint in the pursuit of taste rather than excess. They were, even so, anathema to the evangelical radicalism of reforming middle-class rationality,[4] but at the same time precursors of more general trends in middle-class culture: 'the dandy played an important part in defining modern consciousness – we are all nowadays, to an extent, dandies. . . . Dandyism was an episode in the development of middle-class taste' (Bayley 1991, p. 159). This point has been clarified by the more general development of (although often hailed as an innovation of postmodern culture) individuals who use the design of their personal style as a form of mobile art practice in an aestheticisation of everyday life (Featherstone 1991).

The social phenomenon of dandyism was, therefore, for all its pretensions to aristocratic indolence, a precursor of a bourgeois consciousness, and in this quasi-paradox reminds us of Benjamin's emphasis on the *flâneur* (see Chapter 6) as the spirit of a new urban culture that could not survive in mass society. Although the degree of equivalence between the dandy and the *flâneur*, as English and French representatives of the same phenomenon, is debatable, they did share certain features, such as a commitment to the new public spaces of the growing metropolis and an overriding emphasis on style and taste. The *flâneur*, however, at least in the Baudelaire-Benjamin formulation, is a more tragic figure – fascinated and repelled by the new social masses of the metropolitan era. The *flâneur* also more deliberately haunted the spaces of the emergent consumer society – they inhabited a transitional space between the personal negotiations of pre-modern marketing and the spectacular transformation of public space in the department stores.

The relevance of the *flâneur* to the theme of design in this part of the chapter, and by implication popular lifestyles, can be set out through three interrelated points. (I have been aided in my formulation of these points by the essays collected in Tester (1994).) The first is that the *flâneur* embodies a mode of ironic distancing from the world around himself. Both present and abstracted, the *flâneur* uses his distance to gain a form of control in which he observes and does not participate: 'The *flâneur* epitomises the ideal-type of the citizen . . . an incarnation of a new, urban form of masculine passion manifest as connoisseurship and couched in scopophilia' (Shields 1994, p. 64). I have so far deliberately written of this as a masculine activity; both dandies and *flâneurs* are emphatically male, and yet as the stance becomes popularised it cannot sustain its gendered privilege (although see the painful process of transition described in Wolff (1994)), and becomes a more shared way of using public space.

The third and more general point is then that the stance of the *flâneur* cannot be restricted to its historical specificity and instead must be seen as a more existential or epistemological stance of modernity: '*Flânerie* presupposes an urban epistemology. . . . The inept *flâneur* is derided by Balzac and his contemporaries because he is compelled to act upon what he sees. In other words, the false artist loses the detachment necessary for creativity' (Ferguson 1994, p. 30). I have quoted Ferguson because she brings out well the connection between the ironic detachment and the type of epistemological stance proposed. But in fact she and Benjamin, and Moers in relation to dandies, see these types as historically limited – rendered anachronistic by social change. It is only writers who make the connection to postmodern attitudes who see a more general relevance in their stance: 'To *flâner*, is to rehearse contingency of meaning; life as bagful of episodes none of which is definite, unequivocal, irreversible; life as a play' (Bauman 1994, p. 142; see also Smart in the same collection; and Jenks (1995b) for a more radical version of the *flâneur* as metaphor for sociological vision).

I want then to argue that we can use the social type of elegant artificiality as a model for a more pervasive form of design or consumption work. In this play of reflexivity culture becomes more radically popular as in growing out of everyday practice (see related ideas in Hebdige 1988) than in the conventional orthodoxy of using popular to mean resisting hegemonic control. The aesthetic principles of ironic detachment may be only a refusal – that is a refusal of both face value and an underlying totalising explanation – but in the play of meaning and constant awareness of the instability of representation consumption work can offer a viable sphere for practical aesthetics. It must be the project of lifestyle research to trace all the forms of aesthetic sense in consumption work.

I said previously that I wanted to both broaden a notion of design to include consumption work, and to broaden the notion of work here from purchasing to using material culture. It is in relation to this second aim that we have to look at other aspects of the aestheticisation of everyday life. I have noted that one of the main fields for the exercise of mundane design is in terms of furnishing and decorating households, offices and other living spaces. Of course a new type of professional expertise has developed in relation to interior design, but Bayley has light-heartedly suggested that these experts have and do enjoy the highest status when the components they use are completely arbitrary: 'Americans enjoy interior design for the same reasons they enjoy Coca-Cola ... lost in a vast continent free of any but the most recent traditions, they crave symbols and symbolism' (1991, p. 116). In practice ordinary people cannot afford the advice of interior designers and, while they may consult magazines and furnishing shops, their design choices are necessarily framed within an interplay between their understandings of membership and reference group conventions. Strategies for the design of these interiors, and exteriors such as gardens, yards, etc. will interweave public and private considerations and particular senses of social relevance.

The idea that the everyday use of material culture is always undertaken within a context of received traditions, both local and invented, introduces the possible relevance of a figure such as William Morris in formulating a social aesthetic. Working in the later nineteenth century, William Morris was a prominent socialist activist who believed that industrialisation had destroyed authentic engagement for the greater part of the working population. With his disciples in the Arts and Crafts Movement, they pioneered the use of medieval forms and images in furnishings, textiles and objects, such as the binding and printing of books, which were meant to be an explicit critique of capitalist manufacture. It is frequently argued that his socialist ideals for raising the lived experience of the masses were contradicted by the necessary high cost of his hand-crafted goods that could only be afforded by richer groups. The subsequent history of Morris designs, particularly in textiles and wallpapers, follows an interesting trajectory through various 'layers' of suburban chic during the twentieth century.

The relevance of Morris to the approach developed in this book does not, however, lie so much in the several ways his rather sensual themes have been taken to represent good taste, but in the way his radicalism focuses on the competing relevance of tradition and innovation to a social aesthetic of design. Morris represents the past both because of his historical location and because of the explicit medievalism of his recommendations for practices of production; but, paradoxically, he also represents the future because of his criticisms of mass production. In his concern with the necessity of a truth to materials and the need for an authority of engagement (authorship or creativity by ordinary people) he anticipates central themes in any politics of practical aesthetics.

This is not to say that the dogged non-commercialism of a quest for authenticity, as in for example many aspects of folk music revivals or the preservation of traditional crafts, is an appropriate model. And particularly the ideological blindness of the heritage industry would be hated by Morris. But his values are echoed in many of the thematic values characteristic of green politics such as the need for a sensuous engagement, through qualities such as texture, colour, taste and smell, with the materials and foods and experiences of material culture; the concern to sustain non-exploitative forms of production of both peoples, animals and environments; and a respect for material culture as a multiplicity of living ecologies. These are visible concerns in everyday consumption work, and in their political judgements they do exemplify a notion of design as a way of using that is invested with significance.[5]

Although I think that the relevance of Morris's concern with the principles of good design has been caught up and re-worked in many of the themes that Giddens has characterised as lifestyle politics, this is not the only reason for using him here. The distinctiveness of Morris's radicalism was a refusal to make a principled distinction between public and private spheres as political arenas. In all the different ways we have seen a politics of personal experience, most notably in feminist social thought, come to dominate critical energies, and an adaptation of generally available cultural idioms to local experience – as in the negotiation of ethnic and multicultural distinction in the heterogeneous metropolises of mass society – then lifestyles have been, as I emphasised at the beginning of the chapter, ways of enacting new forms of identity. The creative energies involved in articulating and sustaining new patterns of social association are in a very profound sense a form of design (and require new modes of social expertise in designs for these social politics, see Sennett (1991, especially Part 4)), a way of working with and using the symbolic profusion of material culture in mass society to constitute new cultural forms.

NOTES

1 To give a simple illustrative example – producing a radio or television receiver is not sufficient in itself; the device must be housed in a box on which are inscribed controls, etc. The form of the set may be designed to evoke connotations of modernist minimalism or heavy traditional furniture – what is important is that the technology does not determine its use or meaning but is articulated through a vocabulary of design.

2 Bayley has distilled and summarised the principles of modernist design as

> Respect the nature of materials. Never force unnatural forms or contrived patterns. Wherever possible, choose the simplest and most direct alternative. Ornament is usually reprehensible, but especially so if applied by a machine. Avoid the bogus. Pay attention to the intended functions, which will usually provide a key to the form. Look to nature and to science for inspiration. Respect tradition but do not ape it. Express your intentions honestly and clearly. Ensure that the details harmonize with the whole.
>
> (1991, p. 213)

3 It is important to remember as well that these sources have informed expert discourses that are expressed in lifestyle and home decorating magazines, etc. that are a crucial part of transmitting lifestyle values and aesthetics.

4 And to their spiritual heirs – Marxist intellectuals deploring the insincerity and futility of consumer culture.

5 It may be true that many of those who espouse green values speak from romantic ignorance or do not do so in rational terms (see Witherspoon 1994) but this does not vitiate these struggles with aesthetic principles.

11
Postscript

I believe that in the course of the book I have made clearer some of the ways in which concepts of lifestyle have been used in contemporary social theory and research. I have tried to show the sorts of circumstances for which lifestyles have been seen to be particularly relevant, and I have described the changing contours of lay as well as professional social description in order to indicate the coming cultural forms of social identification. I have in this book argued that the social phenomenon of lifestyles has been an integral feature of the development of modernity, not least in the idea that lifestyles are a particularly significant representation of the quest for individual identity that is also such a defining characteristic of modernity. More generally, I hope to have shown that many of the economic and technical processes that have shaped the development of modern experience have also led to the increasing significance of lifestyles as modes of social association. In this very brief postscript I want to bring out what I believe to be the most important aspect of the discourse of lifestyles for a social theory of modernity.

The era of the modern world has been characterised by the emergence of dominant secular ideologies articulating social conflict based on differing degrees and forms of class consciousness (Gouldner 1976); a search for social explanation that is itself an instance of what Lyotard has famously called the grand narratives of modernity (1984). In addition, two other commonly accepted characteristics have been: the overriding dominance of the nation-state – and the imaginations of community articulated in national-ism (Anderson 1983); and the central notion of a public sphere, based in impersonal rational discourse (Habermas 1989), differentiated from the more feminine, domestic interiors of private experience (Garmanikow and Purvis 1983; McDowell and Pringle 1992). The former notion of the nation-state has been so fundamental to social thought that for the greater part sociological discourse has presumed a practical equivalence between a nation-state and a society. The latter notion of differentiated spheres has underlain the discourse of democratic citizenship, and the social theory of feminism, as well as studies of the public discourses of mass communication and entertainment.

It has, however, become apparent in the course of the progress of the book that lifestyles undermine the initial three character-istics of modernity identified above. In relation to the first I have argued that in their instability and plurality lifestyles resist any incorporation into a grand narrative authoritatively describing social structural forms as an explanation of social discourse. While in relation to the second, it is apparent that production and distri-bution organisations servicing lifestyle concerns by definition tran-scend national boundaries and make a mockery of any notion of national culture – while they do not destroy local experience they cast it into a necessarily dialectical (or ironic) relationship with the spectacular dramaturgy of global industries. And, third and most importantly, that lifestyles have acted to significantly blur, and thus transform, established distinctions between public and private spheres – and in so doing they have acted to inform and constitute new understandings of the relationships between individual and collective forms of social existence.

To the extent therefore that lifestyles, while the child of mod-ernity, also signal the increasing inappropriateness of the basic terms of social discourse (the fundamental intellectual architecture) of that era, they point necessarily towards the need for a recognition of the emergent structural forms of what is literally a post modern era.

Bibliography

Anderson, B. (1983) *Imagined Communities: Reflections on the Origin and Spread of Nationalism*, Verso, London.

Appadurai, A. (ed.) (1986) *The Social Life of Things: Commodities in Cultural Perspective*, Cambridge University Press, Cambridge.

Bailey, P. (1978) *Leisure and Class in Victorian England: Rational Recreation and the Contest for Control 1830–85*, Routledge & Kegan Paul, London.

Banham, R. (1960) *Theory and Design in the First Machine Age*, Architectural Press, London.

Barth, G. (1980) *City People: The Rise of Modern City Culture in Nineteenth Century America*, Oxford University Press, New York.

Barthes, R. (1983) *The Fashion System* (trans. M. Ward and R. Howard), University of California Press, Berkeley.

Baudrillard, J. (1983) *Simulations* (trans. P. Foss *et al.*), Semiotext(e), New York.

——(1988) *America* (trans. C. Turner), Verso, London.

——(1993) *Symbolic Exchange and Death* (trans. Iain Hamilton Grant), Sage, London.

Bauman, Z. (1987) *Legislators and Interpretors: On Modernity, Postmodernity and the Intellectuals*, Polity Press, Cambridge.

——(1991) *Modernity and Ambivalence*, Polity Press, Cambridge.

——(1992) *Intimations of Postmodernity*, Routledge, London.

——(1994) 'Desert spectacular', in K. Tester (ed.) *The Flâneur*, Routledge, London.

Bayley, S. (1991) *Taste: The Secret Meaning of Things*, Faber & Faber, London.

Beardsworth, A. and Keil, T. (1992) 'The vegetarian option: varieties, conversions, motives and careers', *The Sociological Review*, 40(2): 253–93.

Bell, W. (1958) 'Social choice, lifestyles and suburban residence', in W. Dobriner (ed.) *The Suburban Community*, Putnam, New York.

Benjamin, W. (1970) 'The work of art in the age of mechanical reproduction', in *Illuminations* (trans. H. Zohn), Fontana, London.

——(1973) *Charles Baudelaire: A Lyric Poet in the Era of High Capitalism* (trans. H. Zohn), New Left Books, London.

Bensman, J. and Lilienfeld, R. (1979) *Between Public and Private: The Lost Boundaries of the Self*, The Free Press, New York.

——and Vidich, A. J. (1995) 'Changes in the life-styles of American classes', in A. J. Vidich (ed.) *The New Middle Classes: Life-styles, Status Claims and Political Orientations*, Macmillan, London.

Berger, P. L. and Luckmann, T. (1967) *The Social Construction of Reality: Everything that Passes for Knowledge in Society*, Allen Lane, London.

Berking, H. and Neckel, S. (1993) 'Urban marathon: The staging of individuality as an urban event', *Theory, Culture and Society*, 10(4): 63–78.

Berman, M. (1983) *All That Is Solid Melts Into Air: The Experience of Modernity*, Verso, London.

Bernstein, B. (1971) *Class, Codes and Control: Vol. 1, Theoretical Studies Towards a Sociology of Language*, Routledge & Kegan Paul, London.

Blaxter, M. (1990) *Health and Lifestyles*, Tavistock Press, London.

Bocock, R. (1993) *Consumption*, Routledge, London.

Bordo, S. (1993) *Unbearable Weight: Feminism, Western Culture and the Body*, California University Press, London.

Bourdieu, P. (1977) *Outline of a Theory of Practice* (trans. R. Nice), Cambridge University Press, Cambridge.

——(1984) *Distinction: A Social Critique of the Judgement of Taste* (trans. R. Nice), Routledge, London.

——(1991) *Language and Symbolic Power* (ed. J. Thompson; trans. G. Raymond and M. Adamson), Polity Press, Cambridge.

——(1993) *The Field of Cultural Production: Essays on Art and Literature* (trans. R. Johnson), Polity Press, Cambridge.

——and Passeron, J.-C. (1990) *Reproduction in Education, Society and Culture* (trans R. Nice), 2nd edn, Sage, London.

Bowlby, R. (1985) *Just Looking: Consumer Culture in Dreisser, Gissing and Zola*, Methuen, London.

Brake, M. (1980) *The Sociology of Youth Culture and Youth Sub-cultures*, Routledge, London.

——(1985) *Comparative Youth Culture: The Sociology of Youth Cultures and Youth Subcultures in America, Britain and Canada*, Routledge, London.

Brewer, J. and Porter, R. (eds) (1992) *Consumption and the World of Goods*, Routledge, London.

Brint, S. (1984) ' "New class" and cumulative trend explanations of liberal political attitudes of professionals', *American Journal of Sociology*, 90: 30–71.

Bronner, S. J. (ed.) (1989) *Consuming Visions: Accumulation and Display of Goods in America 1880–1920*, W. W. Norton, New York.

Bryman, A. (1995) *Disney and His Worlds*, Routledge, London.

Buck-Morss, S. (1986) 'The *Flâneur*, the sandwichman and the whore: The politics of loitering', *New German Critique*, 39(Fall): 99–142.

——(1989) *The Dialectics of Seeing: Walter Benjamin and the Arcades Project*, MIT Press, Cambridge, Mass.

Bunton, R. and Burrows, R. (1995) 'Consumption and health in the "epidemiological" clinic of late modern medicine', in Bunton *et al.* (eds) *The Sociology & Health Promotion: Critical Analyses & Consumption, Lifestyles and Risk*, Routledge, London.

Bunton, R., Nettleton, S. and Burrows, R. (eds) (1995) *The Sociology of Health Promotion: Critical Analyses of Consumption, Lifestyle and Risk*, Routledge, London.

Burke, P. (1978) *Popular Culture in Early Modern Europe*, Temple Smith, London.

Campbell, C. (1987) *The Romantic Ethic and the Spirit of Modern Consumerism*, Basil Blackwell, Oxford.

Carrithers, M., Collins, S. and Lukes, S. (eds) (1985) *The Category of the Person: Anthropology, Philosophy and History*, Cambridge University Press, Cambridge.

Cauter, L. de (1993) 'The panoramic ecstasy: on world exhibitions and the disintegration of experience', *Theory, Culture and Society*, 10(4): 1–24.

Central Statistical Office (1994) *Social Trends 24*, HMSO, London.

Certeau, M. de (1984) *The Practice of Everyday Life* (trans. S. F. Rendall), University of California Press, Berkeley.

Chambers, I. (1985) *Urban Rhythms*, Macmillan, London.

Chanan, N. (1980) *The Dream that Kicks*, Routledge, London.

Chaney, D. (1972) *Processes of Mass Communication*, Macmillan, London.

——(1979) *Fictions and Ceremonies: Representations of Popular Experience*, Edward Arnold, London.

——(1983) 'The department store as a cultural form', *Theory, Culture and Society*, 3(1): 22–31.

——(1993) *Fictions of Collective Life: Public Drama in Late Modern Culture*, Routledge, London.

——(1994) *The Cultural Turn: Scene-setting Essays in Contemporary Cultural History*, Routledge, London.

——(1995) 'The spectacle of honour: changing dramatisations of status', *Theory, Culture and Society*, 12(3): 147–67.

——(1996) 'Authenticity and suburbia', in S. Westwood and J. Williams (eds) *Imagining Cities*, Routledge, London.

——and Chaney, J. H. (1979) 'The audience for mass leisure', in H.-D. Fischer and S. R. Melnik (eds) *Entertainment: A Cross-Cultural Examination*, Hastings House, New York.

Clarke, J. and Critcher, C. (1985) *The Devil Makes Work: Leisure in Capitalist Britain*, Macmillan, London.

Cohen, E. (1979) 'A phenomenology of tourist experiences', *Sociology*, 13: 179–201.

Cohen, M. (1993) *Profane Illumination: Walter Benjamin and the Paris of Surrealist Revolution*, University of California Press, Berkeley.

Cohen, S. and Taylor, L. (1993) *Escape Attempts: The Theory and Practice of Resistance to Everyday Life*, 2nd edn, Routledge, London.

Connerton, P. (1989) *How Societies Remember*, Cambridge University Press, Cambridge.

Cox, B. D. (1987) *The Health and Lifestyle Survey*, Cambridge University Press, Cambridge.

——, Huppert, F. A. and Whichelow, M. J. (eds) (1993) *Health and Lifestyle Survey: Seven Years On*, Dartmouth, Aldershot.

Crompton, R. (1993) *Class and Stratification: An Introduction to Current Debates*, Polity Press, Cambridge.

Cross, G. (1993) *Time and Money: The Making of Consumer Culture*, Routledge, London.

Csikszentmihalyi, M. and Rochberg-Halton, E. (1981) *The Meaning of Things: Domestic Symbols and the Self*, Cambridge University Press, Cambridge.

Cunningham, H. (1980) *Leisure in the Industrial Revolution*, Croom Helm, London.

Czyzewski, M. (1994) 'Reflexivity of actors versus reflexivity of accounts', *Theory, Culture and Society*, 11(4): 161–8.

Davidoff, L. (1973) *The Best Circles*, Croom Helm, London.

——and Hall, C. (1987) *Family Fortunes: Men and Women of the English Middle Class 1780–1850*, Hutchinson, London.

Davis, F. (1992) *Fashion, Culture and Identity*, University of California Press, London.

Dayan, D. and Katz, E. (1992) *Media Events: The Live Broadcasting of History*, Harvard University Press, Cambridge, Mass.

DiMaggio, P. (1982a) 'Cultural entrepreneurship in nineteenth century Boston 1: the creation of an organizational base for high culture in America', *Media, Culture and Society*, 4: 33–50.

——(1982b) 'Cultural entrepreneurship in nineteenth century Boston 2: The classification and framing of American art', *Media, Culture and Society*, 4: 303–22.

——(1994) 'Social stratification, life-style, and social cognition', in D. B. Grusky (ed.) *Social Stratification: Class, Race, and Gender in Sociological Perspective*, Westview Press, Boulder, Co.

Donald, J. (1993) 'The natural man and the virtous woman: reproducing citizens', in C. Jenks (ed.) *Cultural Reproduction*, Routledge, London.

Dormer, P. (1993) *Design Since 1945*, Thames & Hudson, London.

Douglas, M. (1970) *Natural Symbols: Explorations in Cosmology*, Barrie & Rockliff, London.

——(ed.) (1973) *Rules and Meanings*, Penguin Books, London.

——(1987) *Constructive Drinking: Perspectives on Drink from Anthropology*, Cambridge University Press, Cambridge.

——and Isherwood, B. (1979) *The World of Goods: Towards an Anthropology of Consumption*, Allen Lane, London.

Eco, U. (1987) *Travels in Hyperreality* (trans. W. Weaver), Picador, London.

Elias, N. (1978) *The Civilizing Process*, Volume I, *The History of Manners*, Basil Blackwell: London.

Ewen, S. (1976) *Captains of Consciousness: Advertising and the Social Roots of the Consumer Culture*, McGraw Hill, New York.

——(1990) *All Consuming Images: The Politics of Style in Contemporary Culture*, Basic Books, New York.

——and Ewen, E. (1982) *Channels of Desire: Mass Images and the Shaping of American Consciousness*, McGraw Hill, New York.

Falk, P. (1994) *The Consuming Body*, Sage, London.

Featherstone, M. (1991) *Consumer Culture and Postmodernism*, Sage, London.

——and Turner, B. S. (1995) 'Body and society: an Introduction', *Body and Society*, 1(1): 1–12.

Ferguson, P. Parkhurst (1994) 'The *Flâneur* on and off the streets of Paris', in K. Tester (ed.) *The Flâneur*, Routledge, London.

Feuer, J., Kerr, P. and Vahimagi, T. (eds) (1984) *MTM Quality Television*, British Film Institute, London.

Fiddle, S. (1967) *Portraits from a Shooting Gallery: Life Styles from the Drug Addict World*, Harper and Row, New York.

Finkelstein, J. (1991) *The Fashioned Self*, Temple University Press, Philadelphia.

Fishman, R. (1987) *Bourgeois Utopias: The Rise and Fall of Suburbia*, Basic Books, New York.

Fiske, J. (1989a) *Understanding Popular Culture*, Unwin Hyman, London.

——(1989b) *Reading Popular Culture*, Unwin Hyman, London.

Forty, A. (1986) *Objects of Desire: Design and Society 1750–1980*, Thames & Hudson, London.

Foucault, M. (1977) *Discipline and Punish* (trans. A. Sheridan), Allen Lane, London.

Fowler, B. (1994) 'The hegemonic work of art in the age of electronic reproduction: an assessment of Pierre Bourdieu', *Theory, Culture and Society*, 11(1): 129–54.

Fox, R. W. and Jackson Lears, T. J. (1983) *The Culture of Consumption: Critical Essays in American History 1880–1980*, Pantheon Books, New York.

Fraser, W. H. (1981) *The Coming of the Mass Market 1850–1914*, Macmillan, London.

Frisby, D. (1985) *Fragments of Modernity: Theories of Modernity in the Work of Simmel, Kracauer and Benjamin*, Polity Press, Cambridge.

——(1992) *Simmel and Since: Essays on Georg Simmel's Social Theory*, Routledge, London.

Gaines, J. and Herzog, C. (eds) (1990) *Fabrications: Costume and the Female Body*, Routledge, New York.

Garber, M., Matlock, J. and Walkowitz, R. L. (eds) (1993) *Media Spectacles*, Routledge, London.

Garmanikow, E. and Purvis, J. (eds) (1983) *The Public and the Private*, Heinemann, London.

Geertz, C. (1973) *The Interpretation of Cultures*, Hutchinson, London.

Giaccardi, C. (1995) 'Television advertising and the representation of social reality', *Theory, Culture and Society*, 12(1): 109–32.

Giddens, A. (1990) *The Consequences of Modernity*, Polity Press, Cambridge.

——(1991) *Modernity and Self-Identity: Self and Society in the Late Modern Age*, Polity Press, Cambridge.

——(1992) *The Transformation of Intimacy: Sexuality, Love and Eroticism in Modern Societies*, Polity Press, Cambridge.

——(1993) *New Rules of Sociological Method: A Positive Critique of Interpretative Sociologies*, Polity Press, Cambridge.

——(1994) *Beyond Left and Right: The Future of Radical Politics*, Polity Press, Cambridge.

Gledhill, C. (ed.) (1991) *Stardom: Industry of Desire*, Routledge, London.

Goffman, E. (1959) *The Presentation of Self in Everyday Life*, Penguin, Harmondsworth.

——(1977) *Gender Advertisments*, Macmillan, London.

Goldman, R. and Papson, S. (1994) 'Advertising in the age of hypersignification', *Theory, Culture and Society*, 11(3): 23–54.

Gouldner, A. W. (1976) *The Dialectic of Ideology and Technology*, Seabury Press, New York.

Greenhalgh, P. (1988) *Ephemeral Vistas: The* Exposition Universelles, *Great Exhibitions and World's Fairs 1851–1939*, Manchester University Press, Manchester.

Habermas, J. (1989) *The Structural Transformation of the Public Sphere: An Inquiry into a Category of Bourgeois Society*, Polity Press, Cambridge.

Hall, C. (1992) 'The history of the housewife', in *White, Male and Middle-Class: Explorations in Feminism and History*, Polity Press, Cambridge.

Hall, S. and Jefferson, T. (eds) (1976) *Resistance through Rituals*, Hutchinson, London.

Hanke, R. (1989) 'Mass media and lifestyle differentiation: an analysis of the public discourse about food', *Communication*, 11: 221–38.

Haug, W. F. (1986) *Critique of Commodity Aesthetics: Appearance, Sexuality and Advertising in Capitalist Society*, Polity Press, Cambridge.

Hebdige, D. (1979) *Subculture: The Meaning of Style*, Methuen, London.

——(1988) *Hiding in the Light*, Routledge, London.

Hendry, L. B., Shucksmith, J., Love, J. G. and Glendinning, A. (1993) *Young People's Leisure and Lifestyles*, Routledge, London.

Henry, I. (ed.) (1994) *Leisure: Modernity, Postmodernity and Lifestyles*, Leisure Studies Association, Brighton.

Horowitz, D. (1985) *The Morality of Spending: Attitudes Toward the Consumer Society in America 1875–1940*, Johns Hopkins University Press, Baltimore.

Hunt, L. (1984) *Politics, Culture, and Class in the French Revolution*, University of California Press, Berkeley.

Jackson, A. A. (1991) *The Middle Classes 1900–50*, D. St. J. Thomas, Nairn, Scotland.

Jackson, K. T. (1985) *Crabgrass Frontier: The Suburbanization of the United States*, Oxford University Press, New York.

Jenkins, R. (1983) *Lads, Citizens and Ordinary Kids: Working-class Youth Life-styles in Belfast*, Routledge & Kegan Paul, London.

——(1992) *Pierre Bourdieu*, Routledge, London.

Jenks, C. (1993) 'Introduction: The analytic bases of cultural reproduction theory', in C. Jenks (ed.) *Cultural Reproduction*, Routledge, London.

——(1995a) 'The centrality of the eye in Western culture: an introduction', in C. Jenks (ed.) *Visual Culture*, Routledge, London.

——(1995b) 'Watching your step: The history and practice of the *flâneur*', in C. Jenks (ed.) *Visual Culture*, Routledge, London.

Johnson, P. (ed.) (1994) *Twentieth Century Britain: Economic, Social and Cultural Change*, Longman, London.

Katz, E. and Lazarsfeld. P. (1955) *Personal Influence: The Part Played by People in the Flow of Mass Communications*, Free Press, New York.

Keat, R., Whiteley, N. and Abercrombie, N. (1994) *The Authority of the Consumer*, Routledge, London.

Kellner, D. (1992) 'Popular culture and the construction of post-modern identities', in S. Lash and J. Friedman (eds) *Modernity and Identity*, Basil Blackwell, Oxford.

Kelly, M. P., Davies, J. K. and Charlton, B. G. (1993) 'Healthy cities: a modern problem or a post-modern solution?', in J. K. Davies and M. P. Kelly (eds) *Healthy Cities: Research and Practice*, Routledge, London.

Kephart, W. M. (1982) *Extraordinary Groups: The Sociology of Unconventional Life-styles*, 2nd edn, St Martin's Press, New York.

Kuhn, A. (1985) *The Power of the Image: Essays on Representation and Sexuality*, Routledge & Kegan Paul, London.

Laermans, R. (1993) 'Learning to consume: early department stores and the shaping of modern consumer culture 1860–1914', *Theory, Culture and Society*, 10(4).

Lamont, M. and Fournier, M. (1992) *Cultivating Differences: Symbolic Boundaries and the Making of Inequality*, University of Chicago Press, Chicago.

Lancaster, W. (1994) *The Department Store: A Social History*, Pinter, London.

Langman, L. (1992) 'Neon cages: shopping for subjectivity', in R. Shields (ed.) *Lifestyle Shopping: The Subject of Consumption*, Routledge, London.

Lash, S. (1990) *The Sociology of Postmodernism*, Routledge, London.

——and Urry, J. (1987) *The End of Organized Capitalism*, Polity Press, Cambridge.

——and——(1994) *Economies of Signs and Spaces*, Sage, London.

Lee, M. J. (1993) *Consumer Culture Reborn: The Cultural Politics of Consumption*, Routledge, London.

Leiss, W., Kline, S. and Jhally, S. (1986) *Social Communication in Advertising: Persons, Products and Images of Well-being*, Methuen, London.

Ley, D. and Olds, K. (1988) 'Landscape as spectacle: world's fairs and the culture of heroic consumption', *Society and Space*, 6: 191–212.

Liebergott, S. (1993) *Pursuing Happiness: American Consumers in the Twentieth Century*, Princeton University Press, New Jersey.

Lull, J. (1995) *Media, Communication, Culture: A Global Approach*, Polity Press, Oxford.

Lunt, P. K. and Livingstone, S. M. (1992) *Mass Consumption and Personal Identity: Everyday Economic Experience*, Open University Press, Milton Keynes.

Lury, C. (1993) *Cultural Rights: Technology, Legality and Personality*, Routledge, London.

Lyotard, J.-F. (1984) *The Postmodern Condition: A Report on Knowledge*, Manchester University Press, Manchester.

MacCannell, D. (1976) *The Tourist: A New Theory of the Leisure Class*, Macmillan, London.

McDowell, L. and Pringle, R. (eds) (1992) *Defining Women: Social Institutions and Gender Divisions*, Polity Press, Cambridge.

McKendrick, N., Brewer, J. and Plumb, J. H. (1983) *The Birth of a Consumer Society: The Commercialization of Eighteenth Century England*, Hutchinson, London.

McRobbie, A. (1980) 'Settling accounts with subcultures: a feminist critique', *Screen International*, 34: 37–49.

Malcolmson, R. W. (1973) *Popular Recreations in English Society*, Cambridge University Press, Cambridge.

Marchand, R. (1985) *Advertising the American Dream: Making Way for Modernity 1920–40*, University of California Press, Berkeley.

Markus, T. A. (1993) *Buildings and Power: Freedom and Control in the Origin of Modern Building Types*, Routledge, London.

May, L. (1980) *Screening Out the Past: The Birth of Mass Culture and the Motion Picture Industry*, Oxford University Press, New York.

Mennell, S. (1985) *All Manners of Food: Eating and Taste in England and France from the Middle Ages to the Present*, Blackwell, Oxford.

——, Murcott, A. and van Otterloo, A. H. (eds) (1992) *The Sociology of Food: Eating, Diet and Culture*, Sage, London.

Meyrowitz, J. (1985) *No Sense of Place: The Impact of Electronic Media on Social Behavior*, Oxford University Press, New York.

Michman, R. D. (1991) *Lifestyle Market Segmentation*, Praeger, New York.

Miller, D. (1991) *Material Culture and Mass Consumption*, Basil Blackwell, Oxford.

Mintel (1988) *Special Report: British Lifestyles*, Mintel, London.
——(1993) *Third Age Lifestyles*, Mintel, London.
——(1994) *British Lifestyles*, Mintel, London.
Mitchell, A. (1983) *The Nine American Lifestyles*, Macmillan, New York.
Moers, E. (1978) *The Dandy: Brummell to Beerbohm*, University of Nebraska Press, Lincoln.
Moores, S. (1993) *Interpreting Audiences: The Ethnography of Media Consumption*, Sage, London.
Morley, D. (1992) *Television, Audiences and Cultural Studies*, Routledge, London.
Mukerji, C. (1983) *From Graven Images: Patterns of Modern Materialism*, Columbia University Press, New York.
——(1994) 'Toward a sociology of material culture: science studies, cultural studies and the meanings of things', in D. Crane (ed.) *The Sociology of Culture*, Basil Blackwell, Oxford.
Munt, I. (1994) 'The "other" postmodern tourism: culture, travel and the new middle classes', *Theory, Culture and Society*, (11)3: 101–24.
Nedelmann, B. (1990) 'Georg Simmel as an analyst of autonomous dynamics: The merry-go-round of fashion', in M. Kaern, B. S. Phillips and R. S. Cohen (eds) *Georg Simmel and Contemporary Sociology*, Kluwer, Dordrecht.
——(1991) 'Individualization, exaggeration and paralysation: Simmel's three problems of culture', *Theory, Culture and Society*, 8(3): 169–94.
O'Brien, M. (1995) 'Health and lifestyle: a critical mess?', in R. Bunton *et al.* (eds) *The Sociology of Health Promotion*, Routledge, London.
O'Brien, S. and Ford, R. (1988) 'Can we at last say goodbye to social class?', *Journal of the Market Research Society*, 30(3): 289–332.
Olsen, D. J. (1986) *The City as a Work of Art: London, Paris, Vienna*, Yale University Press, New Haven.
Olszewska, A. and Roberts, K. (eds) (1989) *Leisure and Life-Style: A Comparative Analysis of Free Time*, Sage, London.
O'Neill, J. (1989) *The Communicative Body*, Sage, London.
Painter, C. (1986) 'The uses of art', PhD thesis submitted under the Council for National Academic Awards regulations at Newcastle Polytechnic.
Parr, M. and Barker, N. (1992) *Signs of the Times: A Portrait of the Nation's Tastes*, Cornerhouse Publications, Manchester.

Pred, A. (1994) *Recognising European Modernities: A Montage of the Present*, Routledge, London.

Radway, J. (1987) *Reading the Romance: Women, Patriarchy and Popular Literature*, Verso, London.

Richards, T. (1992) *The Commodity Culture of Victorian England: Advertising and Spectacle 1851–1914*, Verso Books, London.

Rigby, B. (1991) *Popular Culture in Modern France: A Study of Cultural Discourse*, Routledge, London.

Ritzer, G. (1993) *The McDonaldization of Society: An Investigation into the Changing Character of Contemporary Social Life*, Pine Forge Press, Thousand Oaks, California.

Robins, D. and Cohen, P. (1978) *Knuckle Sandwich: Growing Up in the Working-Class City*, Penguin, Harmondsworth.

Rogers, E. M. (1983) *Diffusion of Innovations*, 3rd edn, Free Press, New York.

Rojek, C. (1993) *Ways of Escape: Modern Transformations in Leisure and Travel*, Macmillan, London.

Sandywell, B. (1996) *Logological Investigations – Vol. 1, Phenomenology of Reflexivity*, Routledge, London.

Savage, J. (1990) 'Tainted love: the influence of male homosexuality and sexual divergence on pop music and culture since the war', in A. Tomlinson (ed.) *Consumption, Identity and Style*, Routledge, London.

Savage, M., Barlow, J., Dickens, P. and Fielding, T. (1992) *Property, Bureaucracy and Culture: Middle-class Formation in Contemporary Britain*, Routledge, London.

Schama, S. (1987) *The Embarrassment of Riches: An Interpretation of Dutch Culture in the Golden Age*, Collins, London.

Schivelbusch, W. (1980) *The Railway Journey: The Industrialization of Time and Space in the Nineteenth Century*, Blackwell, Oxford.

——(1988) *Disenchanted Light: The Industrialisation of Electricity in the Nineteenth Century*, Berg, New York.

Schreiber, A. L. with Lenson, B. (1994) *Lifestyle and Event Marketing: Building the New Customer Partnership*, McGraw Hill, New York.

Schudson, M. (1993) *Advertising: The Uneasy Persuasion. Its Dubious Impact on American Society*, Routledge, London.

Sennett, R. (1977) *The Fall of Public Man*, Knopf, New York.

——(1991) *The Conscience of the Eye: The Design and Social Life of Cities*, Knopf, New York.

Shad Jr, J. A. (1990) 'The Groundwork of Simmel's new "Storey" beneath historical materialism', in M. Kaern, B. S. Phillips and R. S. Cohen (eds) *Georg Simmel and Contemporary Sociology*, Kluwer, Dordrecht.

Shields, R. (ed.) (1992) *Lifestyle Shopping: The Subject of Consumption*, Routledge, London.

——(1992a) 'Spaces for the subject of consumption', in R. Shields (ed.) *Lifestyle Shopping*, Routledge, London.

——(1992b) 'The individual, consumption cultures and the fate of modernity', in R. Shields (ed.) *Lifestyle Shopping*, Routledge, London.

——(1994) 'Fancy footwork: Walter Benjamin's notes on *flânerie*', in K. Tester (ed.) *The Flâneur*, Routledge, London.

Shilling, C. (1993) *The Body and Social Theory*, Sage, London.

Shotter, J. (1993) *The Cultural Politics of Everyday Life: Social Constructionism, Rhetoric and Knowing of the Third Kind*, Open University Press, Milton Keynes.

Silverstone, R. (1994) *Television and Everyday Life*, Routledge, London.

Simmel, G. (1971a) 'Fashion', in *On Individuality and Social Forms: Selected Writings* (trans. and ed. D. N. Levine), University of Chicago Press, Chicago.

——(1971b) 'The metropolis and mental life', in *On Individuality and Social Forms: Selected Writings* (trans. and ed. D. N. Levine), University of Chicago Press, Chicago.

——(1971c) 'The transcendent character of life', in *On Individuality and Social Forms: Selected Writings* (trans. and ed. D. N. Levine), University of Chicago Press, Chicago.

——(1978) *The Philosophy of Money* (trans. T. Bottomore and D. Frisby), Routledge & Kegan Paul, London.

——(1991a) 'Money in modern culture', (trans. M. Ritter and S. Whimster) *Theory, Culture and Society*, 8(3): 17–31.

——(1991b) 'The problem of style', (trans. M. Ritter) *Theory, Culture and Society*, 8(3): 63–71.

——(1994) 'The bridge and the door', (trans. M. Ritter) *Theory, Culture and Society*, 11(1): 5–10.

Sklar, R. (1978) *Movie-Made America: A Cultural History of American Movies*, Chappell & Co., London.

Slater, D. (1993) 'Going shopping: markets, crowds and consumption', in C. Jenks (ed.) *Cultural Reproduction*, Routledge, London.

Smart, B. (1994) 'Digesting the modern diet: gastro-porn, fast food and panic eating', in K. Tester (ed.) *The Flâneur*, Routledge, London.

Sobel, M. E. (1981) *Lifestyle and Social Structure: Concepts, Definitions and Analyses*, Academic Press, New York.

Spierenburg, P. (1984) *The Spectacle of Suffering*, Cambridge University Press, Cambridge.

Strasser, S. (1989) *Satisfaction Guaranteed: The Making of the American Mass Market*, Pantheon Books, New York.

Synott, A. (1993) *The Body Social: Symbolism, Self and Society*, Routledge, London.

Tester, K. (1991) *Animals and Society: The Humanity of Animal Rights*, Routledge, London.

——(ed.) (1994) *The Flâneur*, Routledge, London.

Thomas, K. (1983) *Man and the Natural World: Changing Attitudes in England 1500–1800*, Allen Lane, London.

Tiedemann, R. (1991) 'Dialectics at a standstill: approaches to the Passagen-Werk', in G. Smith (ed.) *On Walter Benjamin: Critical Essays and Recollections*, MIT Press, Cambridge, Mass.

Tomlinson, A. (1990a) 'Introduction: consumer culture and the aura of the commodity', in A. Tomlinson (ed.) *Consumption, Identity and Style*, Routledge, London.

—— (ed.) (1990b) *Consumption, Identity and Style: Marketing, Meanings and the Packaging of Pleasure*, Routledge, London.

Turner, B. S. (1984) *The Body and Society: Explorations in Social Theory*, Basil Blackwell, Oxford.

——(1988) *Status*, Open University Press, Milton Keynes.

——(1992) *Regulating Bodies: Essays in Medical Sociology*, Routledge, London.

——(1994) 'Preface', in P. Falk *The Consuming Body*, Sage, London.

Twigg, J. (1983) 'Vegetarianism and the meanings of meat', in A. Murcott (ed.) *The Sociology of Food and Eating*, Gower, Aldershot.

Urry, J. (1990a) 'The "consumption" of tourism', *Sociology*, 24(1): 23–35.

——(1990b) *The Tourist Gaze: Leisure and Travel in Contemporary Societies*, Sage, London.

——(1995) *Consuming Places*, Routledge, London.

Veblen, T. (1924) *The Theory of the Leisure Class*, Viking, New York.

Vidich, A. J. (ed.) (1995) *The New Middle Classes: Life-styles, Status Claims and Political Orientations*, Macmillan, London.

Visser, M. (1991) *The Rituals of Dinner: The Origins, Evolution, Eccentricities and Meaning of Table Manners*, Grove Weidenfeld, New York.

Walters, G. D. (1994) *Drugs and Crime in Lifestyle Perspective*, Sage, London.

Walvin, J. (1978) *Leisure and Society 1830–1950*, Longman, London.

Warde, A. (1990) 'Introduction to the sociology of consumption', *Sociology*, 24(1): 1–4.

——(1994) 'Consumption, identity-formation and uncertainty', *Sociology*, 28(4): 877–98.

Watkin, D. (1977) *Morality and Architecture*, Clarendon Press, Oxford.

Weber, M. (1966) 'Class, status and party', in R. Bendix and S. M. Lipset (eds) *Class, Status and Power*, Free Press, New York.

Weber, W. (1975) *Music and the Middle Class: The Social Structure of Concert Life in London, Paris and Vienna between 1830 and 1848*, Croom Helm, London.

Weatherill, L. (1988) *Consumer Behaviour and Material Culture in Britain 1660–1760*, Routledge, London.

Weinstein, D. and Weinstein, M. A. (1993) *Postmodern(ized) Simmel*, Routledge, London.

Wernick, A. (1991) *Promotional Culture: Advertising, Ideology and Symbolic Expression*, Sage, London.

Whittle, S. (ed.) (1994) *The Margins of the City: Gay Men's Urban Lives*, Ashgate, Aldershot.

Williams, R. (1975) *Drama in a Dramatised Society*, Cambridge University Press, Cambridge.

——(1985) 'The metropolis and the emergence of modernism', in E. Timms and D. Kellet (eds) *Unreal City: Urban Experience in Modern European Literature and Art*, Manchester University Press, Manchester.

Williams, R. H. (1982) *Dream Worlds: Mass Consumption in Late Nineteenth Century France*, University of California Press, Berkeley.

Williamson, J. (1978) *Decoding Advertisements*, Marion Boyars, London.

Willis, P. E. (1977) *Learning to Labour*, Saxon House, Farnborough.

——(1978) *Profane Culture*, Routledge & Kegan Paul, London.

——(1991) *Common Culture*, Open University Press, Milton Keynes.

Willis, S. (1991) *A Primer for Daily Life*, Routledge, London.

Wilson, E. (1985) *Adorned in Dreams: Fashion and Modernity*, Virago Press, London.

——(1988) *Hallucinations: Life in the Post-Modern City*, Radius, London.

Witherspoon, S. (1994) 'The greening of Britain: romance and rationality', in R. Jowell, J. Cutice, L. Brook and D. Ahrendt (eds) *British Social Attitudes: The Eleventh Report*, Dartmouth Publishing, Aldershot.

Wolff, J. (1990) *Feminine Sentences: Essays on Women and Culture*, Polity Press, Cambridge.

——(1994) 'The artist and the *flâneur*: Rodin, Rilke and Gwen John in Paris', in K. Tester (ed.) *The Flâneur*, Routledge, London.

Wynne, D. (1990) 'Leisure, lifestyle and the construction of social position', *Leisure Studies*, 9(1): 21–34.

Zablocki, B. D. and Kanter, R. M. (1976) 'The differentiation of life-styles', *Annual Review of Sociology*, 2: 269–98

Name index

Subject index